Goosetown

Reconstructing an
Akron Neighborhood

OHIO HISTORY AND CULTURE

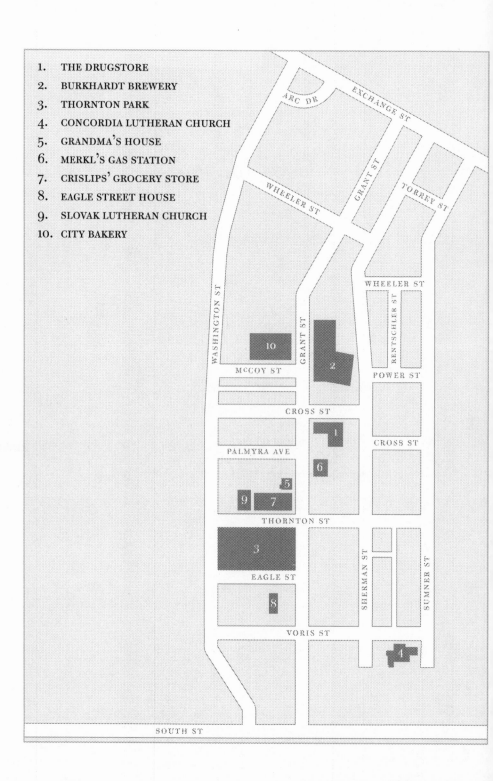

1. THE DRUGSTORE
2. BURKHARDT BREWERY
3. THORNTON PARK
4. CONCORDIA LUTHERAN CHURCH
5. GRANDMA'S HOUSE
6. MERKL'S GAS STATION
7. CRISLIPS' GROCERY STORE
8. EAGLE STREET HOUSE
9. SLOVAK LUTHERAN CHURCH
10. CITY BAKERY

Goosetown

Reconstructing an Akron Neighborhood

Joyce Dyer

The University of Akron Press
Akron, Ohio

18   17   16   15   14   5   4   3

LIBRARY OF CONGRESS CATALOGING-IN-PUBLICATION DATA
Dyer, Joyce.
  Goosetown : reconstructing an Akron neighborhood / Joyce Dyer. — 1st ed.
    p. cm. — (Series on Ohio history and culture)
  ISBN 978-1-931968-70-6 (cloth : alk. paper)
  1. Dyer, Joyce. 2. Dyer, Joyce—Childhood and youth. 3. Early memories—
Ohio—Akron. 4. Neighborhoods—Ohio—Akron. 5. Goosetown (Akron, Ohio)—
Biography. 6. Goosetown (Akron, Ohio)—Social life and customs. 7. Goosetown
(Akron, Ohio)—Description and travel. 8. Akron (Ohio)—Biography. 9. Akron
(Ohio)—Social life and customs. 10. Akron (Ohio)—Description and travel.
I. Title.
  F499.A3D93 2010
  977.1'36—dc22

                    2009041707

ISBN: 978-1-937378-40-0

The paper used in this publication meets the minimum requirements of American
National Standard for Information Sciences—Permanence of
Paper for Printed Library Materials, ANSI z39.48-1984. ∞

Segments of Chapters 9 and 35-37 appeared in *North American Review*,
January–February 2006, in somewhat different form.

Some description of old Goosetown first appeared in "Erratics and Wanderers,"
an essay in *We All Live Downstream* (Motes Books, 2009), edited by
Jason Howard.

All photographs, unless otherwise noted, are courtesy of the author.
Back cover photo: Aerial photo of the Goosetown area prior to 1962. Photo
courtesy of the City of Akron.
Map of Goosetown by Amanda Gilliland.

For Uncle Paul

My heart knows what the wild goose knows,

I must go where the wild goose goes.

Wild goose, brother goose, which is best?

A wanderin' fool or a heart at rest?

—*"Cry of the Wild Goose," Frankie Laine*

PREFACE

When I began work in 2000 on a memoir about growing up in Akron, Ohio, I was quite sure that I would tell the story of both Goosetown and Firestone Park in one book. After all, the two south Akron communities where I lived as a girl were just a little over a mile apart. The same street—Grant—ran through both of them.

It was true that only one chapter in *Gum-Dipped*—and not even the whole of it—ended up being about Goosetown, but that didn't bother me. I recorded the details I could remember. There weren't many, so I filled things in with speculation about how my father might have felt returning to Goosetown after the War and with stories I knew from Akron history about the early days. There wasn't anymore to say.

When we moved from Goosetown to Firestone Park, I was only five years old. So it didn't surprise me that I could barely remember the place.

Oddly, though, Goosetown wanted more space than I had given it. It knew it was more important than half a chapter's worth, even though I did not. It grew insistent. Goosetown kept returning after *Gum-Dipped* was released, like the neglected child it was. In the 1990s I'd begun taking frequent trips back to Goosetown with my uncle Paul, who called himself the "Mayor of Goosetown," even though there wasn't one—and never had been. Maybe it was those trips, and the questions that they raised, that lingered and kept prodding me.

I couldn't get Goosetown back the same way I could Firestone Park, but that didn't mean it wasn't mine. The stories of our lives don't all come through memory, and they don't all come easily. I had to *discover*, not remember, the story of this place. *Find* it. It needed to be told just as much as the other story did. Maybe more.

Goosetown is a story about the *way* that we recover a time in our lives that has nearly vanished. It begins by admitting that we *can't* remember everything about our very early years, and goes from there. The process of reconstructing place and time is the true theme of the book. That process is often as erratic and unpredictable as, well, a wild-goose chase.

It's just as important to admit what you *don't* know about your life as what you *do*. I lived my first five years—the most significant five, some would say—in Goosetown, and I had dismissed them as irrelevant because I couldn't get enough images back. But the years hadn't fled. I just had to find different ways to retrieve them.

Not all of us have Goosetown in our past, but everyone has a shadowy place very much like it that's not clear to them. So I've decided that the best thing I can do is take my readers with me—open the car door and invite them to ride along. Perhaps the ride will help them find their own missing years.

I've chosen to write in the present tense to heighten the illusion of traveling in the present—the way I felt all those years Uncle Paul and I rode through Goosetown together, looking for a place that wasn't even there. My trips with Uncle Paul ended just before 2003, so that's where I end too. Some things have changed on Grant Street since then. But that's all right, because things always change. There's no stopping that.

This book is not an attempt to return Grant Street to the way it was in 1950. Nor to mourn its loss. I'm neither a local historian nor a deeply sentimental soul. Rather, it's a greedy search to find a way to get those lost years back.

SOURCES AND ACKNOWLEDGMENTS

Sources that helped me in my search for Goosetown include *A Centennial History of Akron, 1825-1925*, published in 1925 by the Summit County Historical Society; David W. and Diane DeMali Francis' *Images of America: Akron*, published in 2004 by Arcadia; Karl H. Grismer's *Akron and Summit County*, published in 1952 by the Summit County Historical Society; Scott Dix Kenfield's three-volume *Akron and Summit County Ohio, 1825-1928*, published in 1928 by Clarke; George Knepper's *Akron: City at the Summit*, published in 1981 by Continental; Samuel A. Lane's *Fifty Years and Over of Akron and Summit County*, published in 1892 by Beacon; John S. Murphy, Kathleen A. Kochanski, and Angela K. Schumacher's *Akron Family Album*, published in 2001 by the *Akron Beacon Journal*; Ken Nichols' *Yesterday's Akron: The First 150 Years*, published in 1975 by Seemann; Mark Price's "The Wolf Ledge," published on January 9, 2006, in the *Akron Beacon Journal*; Alissa Skovira's "Goosetown Revisited," published in the September 2004 issue of *Akron Life & Leisure: The Magazine of Greater Akron*; and Abe Zaidan's *Akron: Rising Toward the Twenty-First Century*, published in 1990 by Windsor.

The two sources I relied on most heavily for this book, however, were early issues of the *Akron Beacon Journal* and C.R. Quine's local history, *The Old Wolf Ledge*, published in 1950 as a monograph and reissued in 1958 by the Summit County Historical Society. There is no way to extend sufficient thanks to both *Beacon* reporters who told

the story of Akron's families and WPA workers who indexed issues
from 1841 to 1939. Because of their work, I was able to locate anec-
dotes and information about the Haberkosts and Golzes that helped
me begin to construct the narrative of my own history. And the recollections of Goosetown resident C. R. Quine are invaluable. My book
would be a very different thing without the detail of Goosetown from
the early years that he preserved—including photographs of Goosetown at the turn of the century, descriptions of land formations and
Wolf Run, and lists of residents and businesses.

I thank Tom Bacher, director of the University of Akron Press,
Amy Freels, editorial and design coordinator, and Daniel Von Hol-
ten, editorial assistant, for their helpful comments and good advice
throughout the preparation of this manuscript.

I also am extremely grateful to the staff of the Summit County His-
torical Society; the Summit County Courthouse; the Harold K.
Stubbs Justice Center; local Akron restaurants, especially those on
Waterloo Road; Mount Peace Cemetery; the Municipal Building; the
Morley Health Center; the Holmes County Courthouse; Castle Nurs-
ing Home in Millersburg; and the Ohio Building.

I gratefully acknowledge, as well, the assistance Hiram College
has provided me. Both a sabbatical and Summer Scholar Research
Grant gave me the time I needed to complete this book.

For their especially generous assistance, I would like to thank
Claudia Burdge, planning librarian in the Akron Department of Planning and Urban Development; Chuck Hirsch from the Akron Engi-
neering Bureau; John Miller and Steve Paschen, former archivists at
the University of Akron Archives, as well as the current head of Ar-
chival Services, S. Victor Fleischer; William Hahn, Akron City Arborist and Horticulturalist; Matt Hils, Hiram College professor of biology; George Knepper, premiere Akron historian; Monica and Dave
Hileman, owners of the oldest surviving elm tree in the city who were

kind enough to let Paul Steurer and me spend all the time we cared to in their front yard; Michael G. Prebonick, officer with the Akron Police Department; Wendell Scott, Carol Zink, and Paul Steurer Jr.—my Haberkost family. Most especially, of course, I want to thank Paul Steurer Sr.—the Mayor of Goosetown. I'd give anything to take just one more trip with him for onion soup.

My son, Stephen Osborn Dyer, my daughter-in-law, Melissa McGowan Dyer, and my grandsons, Logan Thomas Dyer and Carson William Daniel Dyer, continue to take care of this good town, and make me proud.

For my husband, Daniel Osborn Dyer, I have no words. This book is as much his as mine.

CHAPTER 1

My eighty-nine-year-old uncle and I are looking for a tree. We're
both staring through the windshield of my Corolla, trying to spot the
lone American elm that survived Dutch elm disease in Akron, Ohio.
An arborist told me about the elm, so I drove twenty minutes from my
house to pick up Uncle Paul. We often go on trips together.

They're not high adventure, but the kind of thing we enjoy.

The arborist said the tree was a hundred feet tall and would be
impossible to miss. Impossible? I've already driven right by the supposed spot and I've only seen a scrawny silver maple.

"Where'd they put it?" he says.

We prowl around Akron every few weeks in search of something. I
drive because Uncle Paul doesn't own a car. An aneurysm in his seventies ended all that. I *do* have a car, but my sense of direction is so
poor that I often get lost, even here, only a mile from where I grew up.

In the end, we usually figure things out. I drive. Uncle Paul di-
rects. Besides, we never go far. We stay near Goosetown, the south
Akron neighborhood where Uncle Paul was raised and where I lived
the first five years of my life. He thinks it's as spectacular as Homer's
Troy. I'm not sure what to think.

Uncle Paul lives on Grant Street. He was born on Grant in 1913 on
the 400th block. He now lives on the 1300th block. Technically, that
part of the street is in Firestone Park—the residential community

both the Steurers and the Coynes moved to in the early 1950s. But Grant Street was the main thoroughfare of Goosetown, so a part of my uncle feels as if he never really left. Goosetown is what defines him. I've lured him away from a Goosetown trip with the promise of seeing the only surviving elm in Akron.

I always buy him onion soup and a piece of pie at a restaurant on Waterloo Road before we start our trips. At lunch today I told him about the tree with a heavy dose of persuasion. He loves trees—always has—but lately he's been so insistent on getting back to Goosetown that I wanted to be as convincing as possible. The minute I mentioned the tree, though, he started eating faster—his signal to get on the road.

Long ago, he'd lost his elms on Ivy Place, a street he lived on with his first wife, Ruth. By the 1960s, every elm in Firestone Park was dead, including the ones on Uncle Paul's devil's strip—the term Akronites use for the patch of grass between the sidewalk and the street.

You'd think a tree as strong as an elm would *never* yield. Sometimes, you still see a lone elm in the middle of a farmer's field, maybe a cow or two under it, enjoying the shade. The elm just wouldn't split, so the farmer left it. Fungi and insects can fell it, though, because its vascular system is so accessible. That's what happened to the Akron elms. I guess you could say it's a tree with too much heart.

The American elm we're looking for stands close to the Ohio Canal. *Just off Waterloo Road a little ways on Ley Drive, near Akron Auto Auction*, the arborist told me. I'm sure I followed the route exactly, but I don't see the tree.

"For a long while we were lucky, and our elms seemed just fine," Uncle Paul says, putting aside the fact we might be lost. Or that maybe the tree doesn't exist. "Our trees ain't gonna get it, I thought. Then I noticed a few yellow leaves one day, and within a week the trees were gone. I didn't know any elms around here lived!"

"Neither did I."

"An American elm," he says, tilting his head even closer to the windshield, with the hope of making the tree materialize. "My, oh, my."

"Keep looking!" I tell Uncle Paul. "It's supposed to be so big you can spot it a mile away."

We squint. We scan the horizon. We coil around Ley and go under the expressway bridge.

"I must have done something wrong," I tell him, and we turn around and head back under the bridge again, toward Waterloo.

"Let's start over," he says. He's used to this. It's why he bought me a compass for my car. I've never figured out how to install it. He glances at the dashtop, and I know he's thinking about the Airguide auto compass he wrapped up for me nearly five years ago as a birthday present, and hasn't seen since. I want to use it. I do. I just can't install it, and my husband isn't any better. I wonder how we survive sometimes.

I always loved the compass my uncle had in his old Fords. I'd watch it bob and spin, then settle somewhere. As a little girl, it was my globe, the whole world divided up into neat grids.

We turn down Ley again, drive a little, and I hear a shout. "There it is, Babe!" my uncle says, pointing to a dark spot in the sky. Now I see it too, the crown of a tree, broad as an open fan, but strangely flat against the sky. Its leaves are dense, and the whole top looks like stage scenery, instead of living cells.

The tree is down a meandering drive, making it impossible to see the elm's trunk from the edge of the road. There's a sign posted—PRI-VATE PARK, NO TRESPASSING, MEMBERS ONLY. We guess the sign is for the park we see off to our left, but we still worry that it might be meant for us. Perhaps we don't belong in the world of this mighty elm. We'll take our chances. I drive slowly. The massive elm swells to fill the windshield, droops into the rearview mirror, and hangs over the sun-roof of the car.

I tell Uncle Paul not to get out yet. I'll go up to the house and see if the owners will let us look at the tree.

A woman with auburn hair answers the door.

"I'm not sure if I'm in the right place, but is that huge tree in your front yard the famous Akron elm?" I ask. I see the wrinkles on her brow begin to climb and a smirk form in one corner of her mouth. She wants to say, "Don't you have eyes," but she doesn't have to.

"All the elms died in our neighborhood fifty years ago," I stumble on. "I haven't seen one in all that time and I've forgotten what they look like."

She nods, but says nothing. Is she sorry for my loss, or for my ig-norance?

"Well, you know, I could be in the wrong place," I blurt.

She finally assures me, in no uncertain terms, I am not.

"It's *magnificent!*" I say.

The woman tells me her name is Monica. She likes me now that I've complimented her tree.

I look over my shoulder and see a yellow coat wobbling toward the elm.

"Be careful, Uncle Paul!" I yell, knowing how unsteady he is on his feet these days. "Wait for me!" He hears me and returns to the Co-rolla, opens the door, and places his hands on the roof, bracing him-self before he swivels in.

Monica leans toward me to see what's going on. She pops back into the house and comes out wearing a light coat. It's a cool spring day.

Monica must sense that Uncle Paul is waiting to hear about the tree, so she doesn't talk again until we collect him from the car. He thanks us both as we walk him toward the elm, never taking his eye off of it.

"I bought the house for the *tree*," she tells us, as we approach its gigantic gray trunk. "This land was the old Ley Turkey Farm. The Leys live all up and down this road. They used to take in boarders. I wanted the tree more than the buildings or even the property," she says.

"An arborist told me Dutch Elm just passed this tree right by," I say.

"A few years ago the tree gave me a scare," she says. "It started to turn yellow, and I panicked. Specialists came out and looked at it and drilled four holes at the base. See them?" She points to the scaly ridges low on the tree's deep bark.

"What are they?" I ask.

"Well, see the pipes they drove into the holes? When they did that, the tubes acted as a kind of spigot and water just whooshed out. Still does. The tree had something called *wet wood*, but it's a lot better for a tree to have that than Dutch Elm."

"Do they still watch the tree?" my uncle asks.

"They tell me it's really a healthy tree, and it's better not to do much else to it. We do keep the pipes in it so it can always drain. We don't even prune it anymore because that attracts beetles and bugs. It's two hundred years old, so everyone sort of feels it's pretty much figured out how to live by now."

My eyes follow the tree from the base of its trunk, where the pipes are, to the large upright limbs supporting the branches that sweep across the sky. There's only solid green as far as I can see. Even on the sides, the foliage surrounds me, branches sagging down like spokes of an old umbrella, its new leaves clinging like heavy fabric. A few dots of light break through. It's daylight, but you'd never know it. Monica watches me.

"It's over fifteen feet in circumference," she says. "The State comes out and measures it every year and gives me a plaque."

The tree is a living time capsule.

"How 'bout that!" my uncle says. He's staring straight up—he can't help himself, even though he knows he shouldn't tilt his neck too far. He'd gotten dizzy in the car just from looking through the top of the windshield. I shouldn't have told him to keep an eye out. I know better. His doctors warned him about looking down or up very far after he had his aneurysm, or turning his head too quickly from side to side. But he never listens if there's something he really wants to see. He doesn't like a diagnosis that limits him in any way. He doesn't want to be an old coach horse constrained by blinders.

He might even be blaming his doctors for having to sell his car after his operation. His second wife became his driver, but then she died, and I was all that he had left—for trips like this. Other people take him to the store and church and doctors' offices, but I'm the only one he's been able to con into driving him to see vanished buildings still vivid to him or to look for old streets and ballfields. When he first called me a few years ago to set out his plan—*to take just a couple of drives through old Goosetown, after a little lunch, of course*—I agreed. He'd practically raised me, so saying "no" would have been like refusing a request from my own dad. Now the trips are so regular I need them to stave off withdrawal. Sometimes, like today, I plan the trips myself and invite my uncle along. If he can't go, I'm always disappointed.

"Jiminy Christmas," he says, tilting even farther back. Monica and I hurry to catch him by his elbows. His legs are wobbling. A fall would be a disaster.

"An American elm right around the corner from me. And it's *two hundred years old.* Why, that's older than me, and I'm older than the Pope!" Loyal Catholic Uncle Paul—ever amazed he outranks the Pope in *something*.

Uncle Paul and the Ley elm

7

I take a picture of my uncle under the tree. He's grabbing it, trying to circle it with his arms, but he has little chance at grasping the entire expanse. Through the lens, flaps of his skin blur with the bark he cuddles up to.

"Do people like us come to see your tree very often?" I ask.

"Sure," Monica says. "Adults come, neighborhood children, school kids. I sometimes tell them, 'Just think. It was here when Commodore Perry was alive!' Before they leave this spot, I want to make sure they know the oldest living thing on the earth is a tree."

Commodore Perry. Battle of Lake Erie. Defeated the British. Eighteen something, wasn't it? I'd learned about him in Ohio history in junior high, but I can't remember much.

We notice all the stonework and planting Monica has done around the large yard surrounding the tree's enormous trunk.

"See all that?" she asks. "I plant and poke here all the time. But do you know that in all the years I've worked this land I've never hit a root of that old elm? I dig and dig. Elm roots aren't supposed to be that deep, but these are. I've never found a single one. They're way out there." She points in the distance, somewhere in the direction of the Firestone factories and Firestone Park.

She points all the way to Goosetown, just north of the Park. I see my uncle wink, and know that he's following the roots of the elm down Grant Street, probably all the way to his boyhood house.

I worry that I'm wearing out my welcome, even though Uncle Paul has charmed his way into Monica's heart. He often manages to do that to people—as long as they have a sense of humor and like his corny jokes.

Monica and Uncle Paul are standing arm in arm under the tree now, talking together like old friends while I snap photographs. No matter how far I move away from the elm, I can't seem to fit it in the camera's frame, and I don't have a wide angle lens.

"I better go!" she says. "Stay as long as you want and come back anytime."

"Thank you," I tell her. Uncle Paul and I head for the car.

As she walks toward her house, Monica raises her arm in the air and quickly rotates her hand at the wrist, waving to us. She looks like a figure on a weathervane.

We back out. Uncle Paul asks me to lower his window so he can wave. Automatic windows baffle him. I'm sure he'll never figure them out. I've tried to teach him how to press the button on his armrest, but he never learns. He just smiles and waits for me to push the master switch.

I tell him Monica has already gone inside, but he doesn't stop. His hearing and sight aren't very good anymore.

He waves and waves until the tree disappears in the rearview mirror. He tells me to roll the window up.

He wants to visit Goosetown before I take him home. He has to walk his dog at 3:00 P.M., so we have to hurry. I turn north off Waterloo until we come to my uncle's street. London Planetrees now line both sides of the two blocks of Grant that lie in Firestone Park, but today I see only the elms that were there.

We follow Grant out of the Park and begin our short drive to Goosetown. I realize I can't even recall if there were trees on the lots of the old neighborhood where both Uncle Paul and I were born.

CHAPTER 2

How do I write this book? How do you retrieve time from a half-century ago? *Can* the past be reclaimed? If Uncle Paul had shown me a large elm in Goosetown when I was a child, like the Ley Elm, would I even have remembered it?

My recollections of elementary school and high school return to me without much effort. I can replay those films. They're easy to dislodge, still catalogued in the crevices of my brain. But the movies of Goosetown are silent. There's so little I remember.

I've read memoirs in which writers record page after page of dialogue from when they were two years old. They know what they ate in their highchairs and can analyze the motives of adults who were spooning pap into them. Their memories are rich and complete. The films of their lives never break, sputter, or need a splice.

I don't believe them. They're lying, or their brains developed in a different way than mine.

The place of memory for me is Firestone Park, not Goosetown. Yes, Goosetown was just a short distance from Firestone Park, but the two places may as well have been on opposite coasts. Only recently have I begun to understand that it was *time*, not distance, that created the immense separation in my mind.

I was barely conscious when I lived in Goosetown, though I took my first steps there. Perhaps there was something that resembled memory struggling to emerge in me, but I don't have a name for it, and I don't even know what areas of my brain contained it. The world passed in front of me in rapid frames, and my eyes fluttered too quickly to record much of anything. But sometimes sensations intruded and slowed things down. They pricked my skin or kept my eyes open for a longer time. Certain things became larger than they really were. Magnified.

Maybe that's why children like cartoons so much. Cartoons are nearly identical to what children see when they step outside. The buildings on their streets are huge shapes against the sky, each one recognizable from its angles or mass. Small objects can take up enormous space too. A dandelion pod waiting to be blown can make a child think her breath is the breath of God, and a neighborhood crow might darken the whole world for her when it flies overhead. To a small child, each person can be distilled into a single trait as indelible as a signature: a long nose, a curl of hair, a bow tie, a cigarette dangling from a mouth, heart-shaped lips like my aunt Marie's.

How can I tell a story without memory? What does a story even look like without memory moving it along?

In my imagination, Goosetown is a dark, forlorn place. My uncle Paul has asked me to write a book about it for years. He says Goosetown has *potential*. But potential for *what*? Potential, perhaps, to call my life into question?

That's what frightens me. I like to say, *I know who I am.* I'm not sure if I'm ready to discover things that throw me off balance. I like the balance I keep. It gives me confidence to know myself as well as I think I do. If I look up or down too quickly, will I teeter and fall, like my uncle?

I *do* admit I sometimes feel as if I'm floating just a few inches above the ground, but not like a ghost, or anything ethereal. When this happens, I'm not completely comfortable. I feel lightheaded and dizzy, the way I am when I'm in ill-health. I seem to hover unsteadily just a short distance above the earth, but I can't touch ground.

The gap could be the forgotten years, the small piece of time that ticked off in Goosetown and then fell away. I think this little bit of room between my feet and the ground is like the blank space between the numbers on a clock—the eight and the nine, for instance, or the twelve and the one. If you were sixty years old, the years of your life could be measured in five-minute intervals by the hands on a clock. On a large kitchen clock, the first five years would be separated by approximately one inch of white, as would every five years after.

If I could somehow push the minute hand back to the twelve, and watch it slowly sweep toward one again, I would have Goosetown back, and I think the dizzy spells would stop.

CHAPTER 3

But how do you do something like that? I'm not a part of Goosetown the way my uncle Paul is. So much of it is gone that it's hard to
even find anymore.

Uncle Paul will never forgive the city for building an expressway
through Goosetown in the 1950s. The construction demolished some
of Princeton Street, where he and Ruth rented a house. An overpass
crosses the freeway about where his house once stood.

He talks with similar derision about the Grant Street–Washington
Street Urban Renewal Project of the 1960s and the expansion of that
project north from Thornton to Palmyra in the 1970s—the leg of construction that leveled my grandma's house. I'm not sure he was very
affected by the Civil Rights Movement or the Women's Movement or
the Vietnam War, but he certainly knew how to protest the destruction of his neighborhood. He wrote letters and visited City Hall, but
it didn't do any good. He watched the bulldozer remove it all—his
house on Princeton Street, every home on Eagle Street (including the
one my parents rented shortly after I was born), and the house at 624
Grant where my Haberkost grandparents resided and where generations of Haberkosts had been raised before August and Anna moved
in as newlyweds in 1904. Thornton Park went too. The only place in
Goosetown I remember seeing trees.

Year after year, cranes demolished most of Uncle Paul's old neighborhood and dump trucks hauled it away. I didn't observe any of this
happening, but Uncle Paul did. He felt the blow of every wrecking
ball.

I noticed all the changes only when I started driving back with
him a few years ago, and everything was gone. Not *everything*, really,
but so many landmarks had been razed that I had lost most of my
moorings.

The story of this place seems so much more Uncle Paul's than
mine, even though there are cells from my body mixed in with Goosetown's soil.

Paul Steurer has been completely shaped by a single road. The
bends in my uncle's legs and back come from the shortcuts he took
through the Burkhardt Brewery lot, the wagon he pulled as a boy, the
paper he reached for every day on his front porch, the flag he lifted
into place every morning for fifty years. The cancers on his skin
formed here too, while he was playing Geese-Geese in the open fields
with his friends or helping his mother weed her vegetable garden on
hot summer days. Even the arches of his feet formed on Grant, on the
small front yards and on the remnants of rocky ledges that were here
when he was young, though most of Goosetown's caves and ravines
had been filled in by then—with level ground for new houses, made
from the dirt of old foundations, from broken towns, from lost farms
and great trees, from someone else's dreams.

My uncle *is* Goosetown, and he knows it.

I wish he'd stop saying that I'm Goosetown too.

CHAPTER 4

What do you remember, Babe?

That's what Uncle Paul asks me every time we set out on a trip. Usually I hear the question halfway between Waterloo Road (where all my uncle's favorite restaurants are) and South Street, Goosetown's southern edge.

Every so often the *Akron Beacon Journal* sends someone out to interview my uncle because a new editor thinks the name *Goosetown* sounds quaint and would make a good story. Here's the way he maps it out for reporters: *Straight down Grant Street from Exchange to South, and a few blocks over on either side.* He's south Akron's most famous cartographer. The only one, really.

That's his official definition for the press, but not the one he really lives by. He's gotten in the habit of calling the blocks of Grant that spill into Firestone Park "South Goosetown." I have, too. He says when the city scooped up old Goosetown, he sorted through the rubble and took its heart with him to the Park. He even uses address labels with "The Heart of Goosetown" printed on the top line.

He tells reporters about the original German settlers who kept geese in their front yards in the nineteenth century and about how those birds served as watch dogs and squawked strangers away. It was Akron's first ethnic neighborhood, he says, with German bands and clubs and halls and charities. He sang with the Akron *Liedertafel* and his wife and my mother were gymnasts at the *Turnerbund*. There was even a German newspaper for a while—the *Akron Germania*. He's always liked words, so he's tried hard to keep the name of his old neighborhood alive. The other guys in the rubber shops talked about the West Virginia neighborhoods they came from—Hill 17, Possum Creek, Whoop'n'Holler—and he wanted to brag about his birthplace. Some people found the name Goosetown offensive—a sort of ethnic slur—but Uncle Paul never did.

Here's what I tell him when he asks me what I remember: *I remember the fence in my backyard on Eagle Street that I pulled myself up on when I began to walk, the tin can the neighbor boy hurled into my forehead, the lesson about hell I learned with Eddie under the windowsill of the church that stood behind Grandma's house, our trips to Portage Lakes, the day that Eddie died, Crislips' Grocery Store on the south side of Grandma's house, a brick building on the north, the Burkhardt Brewery, City Bakery, the Lutheran church we attended on Sumner and Voris, the swimming pool in Thornton Park, Merkl's Gas Station, the drugstore on Cross and Grant.* It doesn't add up to much, I tell him. He just looks at me.

Sometimes, I wonder if I really remember even the few things I *say* I do. I found the picture of the fence on Eagle Street in an old scrapbook of my mother's, so maybe I recall only the photograph, not the memory at all. I like the image of learning to walk by pulling myself up on a fence, so of course I would retain it, and perhaps make more of the photo than was really there. The image anticipates the danger of growing up in a place as hard as Rubber Town, so it supports what I believe really happened to me. Our house was among the second tier of houses constructed in the backyards of Eagle Street to accommodate workers brought to Akron during boom years. We rented one of them. There were no trees or bushes between properties—only wire fences. At least, I have no memory of anything green.

Author uses the fence to learn to walk in the backyard of the Eagle Street house

The lid that flew into my forehead is my most vivid memory of Eagle Street. I've written about the lid before. Such a small thing, yet its meaning changes slightly every time I consider it. The story ages, as I do.

The lid struck me so hard that my mother couldn't stop the blood. It was the first time I saw what was inside of me, and perhaps the first hint I had that whenever what's inside is forced out, there's enormous pain. I remember the reaction of my own small son when he saw a diagram of the organs and skeleton of a bird in a book we brought home from the library. He was curious about it, but also vaguely repelled. You know the truth of pain that's inside even when you're young— know it's connected to blood and bone. Later, you know pain is also caused by the messy secrets buried in your heart.

I was taken to the hospital and given shots and stitches. I still carry a small ridge of skin just behind my hairline from that day. Even a child has little choice but to remember such encounters with mortality. They remain there to frighten us, to remind us, for the rest of our lives. The first encounter is the most startling because the world is never the same again.

I name other encounters here: choking on a lettuce leaf when I was ten years old and being turned upside down and rescued by Uncle Paul, lying with scarlet fever for days in a dark room—drapes drawn, lights out, windows closed—while my heart withered a little in my chest, being told after delivering my son that I was very ill and that my child was ill, too ("Don't worry! He has a 50/50 chance!"), waking up one morning too dizzy to rise and being rushed off in an ambulance, being hit head-on by a spinning car and feeling my sternum crack, seeing blood swirling in a toilet bowl when it had no business being there. When mortality walks in and greets you, he offers his hand. Something in his cold grasp tells you, even when you're three years old, that he's going to return. You haven't seen the last of him.

I can't recall much else, except for a few details of buildings—the funny nose of the drugstore on Cross and Grant, the brick of the brewery, the pouchy screen door on my grandma's house. When I was a girl, I read the day by those prominences. Not by a clock, not even by light, the way the flowers and trees know spring has arrived. Buildings up and down the street were my compass points.

There were the short trips to Crislips' Grocery Store throughout the morning for fruit and candy, colas waiting for us in the middle of the day at Merkl's Gas Station, ice cream at night at the drugstore, church on Sundays with my grandma and my aunts in the Haberkost pew. There was our house on Eagle Street and Grandma's house on Grant, a street away.

If a *Beacon Journal* reporter interviews me one day to find out where Goosetown is, I'll say: *It's between a brewery, a drugstore, a Lutheran church, my grandma's house, and Thornton Park.* He'll be confused because it doesn't look that way anymore, so I'll say one more thing: *If you want to find it now,* I'll tell him, *go to the corner of Grant and Thornton, look up, shield your eyes and your forehead, and watch for a tin can spinning in the vicinity of the new post office. That's where Eagle Street used to be. You're in the heart of Goosetown now.*

CHAPTER 5

I don't think a reporter will ever ask me about Goosetown. It's Uncle Paul they want.

No one can listen to me talk about the little bit I remember and really think that I'm the kind of expert my uncle is.

I'm driving to Goosetown alone today. I haven't told Uncle Paul. I need to see if there's any way I can write the book my uncle wants me to get down *before it's too late*, as he puts it. (He'd probably like it dedicated to him too!) The book has to be mine, as well as his, if I'm going to write it. I have to get tangled up in its threads, or it won't be any good. That much I know. It's for me to decide.

I'm going to drive the entire length of Grant Street—from the two southernmost blocks in Firestone Park where my uncle lives, to Exchange Street on the north, where Grant ends. *Then* I'll make up my mind.

I look straight ahead when I pass his house. Even out of the corner of my eye I can see the tip of his oversized flag waving in the wind. He's home. That's what the flag means. He wouldn't like to know I'm driving on Grant without him, so I slump down a little in my seat.

It's a two-mile trip. That's all there is of Grant.

I want to jar loose something that might be lodged inside my brain. *Anything.* Maybe some bump in the road or unexpected shadow at the corner of a building will wake up my dead nerves. Perhaps

Uncle Paul, with Ginger and his American flag, on his Grant Street porch

some sensation will recharge the circuits in my head and bring more of Goosetown back to me.

I head north across Archwood. I'm out of Firestone Park.

I'm approaching the former Southern Theater on the corner of Cole and Grant. It's the Southern Tap Room now, but I still see myself standing with some friends waiting for the doors to open so a woman can take the coins I'm holding in my hand. We run inside—buy the popcorn and candy—wait for the newsreel, the cartoons, the serial, the cowboy who sings.

Farther down, lit with neon signs, are Amedeo's Florist and DiFeo Poultry. We ordered flowers for the dead at Amedeo's and turkeys to feed the living at DiFeo's. Both businesses are still there, and I remember the small cards my mother let me sign, and the noise and blood of the birds. Even from the Goosetown years there's a memory left: the little bear we chose in the flower shop for my cousin Eddie's coffin. Flower arrangements always meant death in my home. My father never bought my mother romantic gifts, and never purchased a planter or bouquet for her. Not a single rose. But his love was unfailing. My father knew about true passion, but I, his daughter, have often been fooled by the idea of a rose in some man's hand.

I think about Eddie, about his accident. It was explained to us so generally. He was hit by a car, and then he died. That was all there was. So we bought the bear, and his sister, Carol, placed it in Eddie's folded arms. Then, Eddie vanished from Goosetown. I've had to explain death many times now to the young—to my own son, to students—and I really wonder if I've done a better job than my family did explaining it to me. I've tried, but I don't know if it's even possible to talk about death. In the Haberkost family, the obligation to the dead was to keep them dead. You buried them in the ground, and you didn't dig them up. All the adults went on with their lives, and Eddie never appeared again in our sentences.

We moved shortly after Eddie died, and I made new friends in Firestone Park. Eddie had been my best friend—just three months my junior—but after we left Goosetown, Cindy and Mary and Donald took his place.

He's suddenly back in my thoughts as I travel down this road. Or, maybe I never really forgot him.

We had a secret, Eddie and I. I must have thought about it many times during my girlhood, because I still remember it. Maybe after

Goosetown, and after Eddie died, there were signals that triggered it: the onset of night; costumes on Halloween; the pastor lifting his robed shoulders up in the high podium of Concordia Lutheran Church, his head falling forward, the way a vulture's might.

The Slovak Lutheran Church behind my grandma's house was often lit at night for prayer meetings, so Eddie and I would gather near it, like June bugs. The boy who spoke to us that night was not the boy who threw the tin can at my head, but he was the same kind of boy.

I can still see his sharp face. He had a riveting manner and told Eddie, me, and all the other children who gathered there about the fate that awaited us in hell.

"Do you pee your pants?" I remember the boy asking us. Most of us were five or six, and he must have known we did. I don't remember if we answered him.

"If you do," he said, "a red devil is going to come for you." I remember that he described the devil as a monster with red fish skin, horns, and a black pitchfork so fierce that its tines could skewer three children in a single thrust.

Killing us wasn't even the worst of it. The red fish would take us to hell, poked right through the belly, then bring us back to life and put us in a fire that was so hot we'd wish we were dead again, but not quite hot enough to really kill us for good. We would smell burning flesh and sizzling hair, but all we could do about it was scream or throw up. Our eyes would hurt a hundred times worse than when you got soap in them, or bugs under the lids, but we still would see out of them well enough to watch our friends jerking around in the flames like spastics, or electric wires.

Eddie and I held each other's hands as the boy talked, and did pee our pants right there under the sill of the church.

We ran home, but never told anyone about the boy by the Slovak Lutheran Church. It was our secret. We had to get through this together and we knew it, even though we did not know how. I don't think we had any idea what had happened to us that night or why we were afraid. We stayed a little closer to the boundaries of Grandma's house after that, and to each other. Then we stopped talking about the devil with the red fish skin. It was still our secret, but we were happy again.

I think the great sadness of Eddie's death—his life cut short—never registered with me when I was young. What did register was that he had left me alone with a horrible secret. I knew there was no one else to tell once my cousin was gone.

When you're five, secrets that have to stay inside are as dangerous as pitchforks pointed at your heart.

I slow down at a sharp bend in the road, and think I see Eddie's face in the halo of a streetlight. I cross some railroad tracks.

I see the Borden building, and remember an elementary school field trip there. The name of the building is still on the front, carved in stone. But milk isn't processed inside Borden anymore. When I look at it, I still see the cows we drew and studied in second grade; the tall glass of milk my father drank each night before he went to bed; the milkman who drove a white truck and delivered cold milk to my uncle's door in the Park each morning with the handle of his carrier wrapped tightly around his one good arm; the syrup my aunt Ruth sometimes let me stir into white milk; the Elsie cow trivia Uncle Paul taught us—Elmer was her husband, Beulah and Beauregard were her children. There was also the jingle Uncle Paul made us say every time we passed the building or took a drink of milk—*if it's Borden, it's got to be good.* Uncle Paul would tell us that cows came in colors and gave milk that matched their hide—white, strawberry, chocolate. His own son was a born scientist, and just laughed at his father when he said things like this. But Uncle Paul had me looking for brown cows and

Concordia Lutheran Church on Voris and Sumner

white cows and pink cows all over the countryside. I was sure they existed. After all, he said they did.

After I cross South Street, I drive over a bridge that covers the expressway. I hear the noise of traffic below.

If I were to turn right on Voris, shortly after the bridge, I'd quickly arrive at the Lutheran church the Haberkosts attended.

Concordia Lutheran was *our* church. I don't mean we felt that way because we were avid members. (The Haberkosts *were* avid

members.) I mean my family *built* the church. My grandma's brothers, owners of Golz Concrete Block Company, were the general con-
tractors. Everyone was proud of that, and I heard about it almost every Sunday. My grandmother's family, the Golzes, had come from
Massow, Germany. Proud stonemasons. They hauled rock for the
church from local quarries, and also laid the brick. Albert Anton
Koehn, the husband of Anna's sister, did the roofing and sheet metal
work. One of Grandpa's cousins—a Haberkost—married the first
minister of Concordia Lutheran. Another Haberkost was Concordia's Sunday school superintendent for a while. Anna, my grandma,
was a member of Concordia's Forty Year Club. Even Grandpa was a
member of the congregation, though I don't remember ever seeing
him sit in the Haberkost pew. It was the church where my parents
were married, the church where I was baptized, confirmed, and married, too. My cousin Carol still sings in the Concordia choir.

Akron's Main Post Office covers Eagle Street and Thornton Park,
though its official address is Wolf Ledges Parkway, the street just west
of Grant.

Nothing seemed to change when I was young, but now change
seems so rapid that I grab the wheel of my car and hold on tight, ex-
pecting to be swooped up in some great vortex that will spin my few
remaining memories from my head, leaving me as empty of knowl-
edge as an orphan child.

But the roadbed feels familiar. I let it steady me.

Grant is commercially zoned these days. Most shops were located
in the homes of our neighbors in the 1940s and 1950s, not in retail
centers like the ones now clustered on the street. Businesses crawl
north along both sides of Grant from Thornton Street all the way to
Exchange—the last quarter mile of the road. On the west side, Summit Paint and Decorating and B & R Auto Paint Company are about
where Grandma's house and Crislips' Grocery Store used to be.

Around the corner on Thornton, where the Slovak Lutheran Church sat in the 1950s, the Buckeye State Credit Union now stands. Zippy's Pizza occupies the lot just across the street from Grandma's where Merkl had his gas station. There are college apartments on the east side now, as the University of Akron creeps from its downtown center. Keeping an eye on the west side of Grant—Grandma's side—and moving north toward Cross, I see an auto electric shop and the administrative building for the post office.

There's a small parking lot on the west now, at the corner of Cross and Grant. I pull in. This intersection marks the lowest point on the street. Wolf Run, a south Akron stream, carved the contours of Goosetown during the post-glacial age. Before the stream was buried underground, it ran from Spicer Street to the old Ohio & Erie Canal. It formed from source forks at Horix Pond and the old Sumner farm (where a school stands now). The brooks met at Spicer, widened into Brown's Pond, narrowed and traveled through the Allyn Street culvert, passed under Sumner Bridge, and then flowed straight through the Sherman Street culvert into Goosetown.

Cross and Grant is where it made its most dramatic cut and left its deepest impression.

I've never really wanted to explore this corner before, but today I stop. This is the corner where Eddie was struck. The location of his accident was the only specific piece of information we were ever given about his accident. Afterwards, the Haberkosts were adamant about the danger at Cross and Grant because they feared that another child might be lost here. No one could bear to think of another loss, so they warned us, and then warned us again. My family might as well have put up a roadblock, a sign with skulls and crossbones painted on it with the words "Eddie died here."

After Eddie passed away, I don't remember going to the drugstore on Cross and Grant for ice cream again. We moved shortly after his accident, so maybe that's why I stopped. After I grew up, I even avoided driving down Grant Street because of my aversion to "Eddie's" corner. It was irrational, but I had come to believe that just driving over the spot could harm me. I'm not a superstitious person, but childhood fear often transforms into inexplicable lifelong dread.

I've thought about the corner a little more on my trips with Uncle Paul. I've had to. Often he insists on going all the way down Grant, so I have no choice except to drive through the intersection. When we do, Uncle Paul always nods his head in the direction of the building that stands there and says, *That's where Eddie was hit.*

Uh-huh, I say.

I feel uneasy when I leave the car and stare at the building across from me. Eddie was on his way to get a Popsicle at the drugstore. In a folder of my mother's, I found a yellowed clipping from the *Akron Beacon Journal* about his accident. The headline mentions the Popsicle: "Crosses Street for Popsicle, Dies Under Car."

But it's not just what the building *was* that makes me restless now—what it meant in Eddie's life, I mean—but what it *is*.

Today it's a topless bar, the Bottoms Up Lounge. I've heard about this place, read about it in the paper. There are strippers who give lap dances—even during lunch, someone told me. I'm afraid a policeman will see me staring at the building and arrest me for something—vagrancy, voyeurism, indecency, I don't know. What if he thought I was applying for a job? I tighten the scarf around my neck. I feel lewd being here—but I don't know if it's the closeness to sex or to death that disturbs me more. How could I explain this to the officer?

I cross the street—the one that Eddie never finished crossing that hot day in the early 1950s. I'm very nervous as I get closer to the building. It was a sort of pharmacy and general store then, but we always called it a drugstore. The brick of the building is painted red now—no longer natural, the way I remember it.

The old drugstore at Cross and Grant

I want to look inside, but I can't. The windows are all bricked up. The front door too. Some of the windows on the second floor are still intact—opened half-way. All I can see when I squint and try to look inside is the tail of a curtain sneaking out, like someone's nightshirt. Nothing else. No people.

I move to the side of the building and see a woman entering from the parking lot. She's twirling a G-string round and round the index finger of one hand, and with the other patting the hairline of her up-do—ringlets and a ballerina bun. On the wall that faces the customer parking lot is a large mural of a sexy woman bent over so far you can see the bare cheeks of her buttocks and the dark tops of silk stockings that reach to her upper thigh. She's bent like a hairpin and looks back at me over her shoulder. I'm startled. I'd never noticed her before on my drives down Grant with my uncle Paul. How could I have missed her? She looks a little like the woman on the outside wall of Tony's Badda Bing nightclub in *The Sopranos*.

As different as the Bottoms Up Bar is from the drugstore it used to be, it's still shaped like a locomotive, with a pointy nose on its front face that reminds me of a cowcatcher. Even the grillwork of the balcony accentuates this resemblance. I've looked at an aerial photo of this street, and the triangular shape of this building makes it immediately identifiable. At any time in the building's history, my eye would be able to spot this Grant Street landmark.

From the intersection—the basin of the street—the buildings creep north uphill. The old Burkhardt Brewery is next, on the same side of Grant as the Bottoms Up Lounge. I walk over the bricks of Cross Street to see it. I look both ways.

The name is still on the stones above the doors, just like the Borden building, but the stonemason who built the brewery carved a horse's head. Burkhardt sold to the Burger Brewing Company in 1956. Tom Burkhardt opened a brewpub south of Akron decades later, bringing the name back to town for a while, but even the pub is gone now. Burger left Akron in 1964, and the Akron Board of Education eventually purchased the abandoned buildings.

As interesting as the building's history is, I don't think it tells everything. There are so many other stories that no one knows. Buildings, after all, are the theaters where our lives play out. We hold the old playbills in our hands. We know where we were when scenes were performed. We see the rooms where we said our lines.

I remember the small room in the upstairs of our Tudor house in Firestone Park. My mother, Annabelle Coyne, called it the Powder Room. On a kidney-shaped table with a glass top and a ruffled skirt rested her peach Coty powder, her red lipstick, and her silver brush. When my mother went downstairs, I would spread the panels of the skirt and climb under the table (first removing the tiny stool where Annabelle sat as she stroked her hair). There I would pat her powder puff on my cheeks (trying not to cough) and paint my lips like hers. I knew I couldn't stay long—it was risky there—but my mother had no secrets that I could ever find, except in this room, and I wanted to know what they were.

I also remember the kitchen at an aunt's house in New York where a boy's bare knee touched my own and made me lose all appetite except for him; the rooms where things were broken in a rage; the closet where my mother hid when she began to lose her mind; the floorboard in our Church Street house where my husband pressed his knee and held my hand; the study that was too cold, another that was too hot, and the one I occupy now that's too dark and looks out on a funeral home.

The brewery contains stories of generations of workers who have passed through this town. People must have said both wise and hateful things inside, cursed their fate, celebrated births, made up jingles to lessen monotony, decided to leave spouses and children and walk away from this town, fainted from heat and long hours, remembered Germany and Hungary, taken sick, stood outside for factory photographs with a keg and mugs of beer. It's just old scenery now, and that's what makes a vacant building sad. It's as if the houselights have come up—harsh and unforgiving. All the drama and adventure are gone.

This building must hold some small part of me. I must have seen it almost every day of my first five years.

I look at the front of the old brewery and think of Grandpa. He always had a beer in one hand and a smoke in the other. He wore bright white shirts—in summer and winter—with the sleeves rolled up. When he wasn't rocking in the parlor, he was on his porch staring across the street. That's all I can remember about the man. But, strangely, he returns when I stare at the bricks in front of me.

There's only one other person I associate with this brewery. It was also a man, but a very, very young man—a boy I met in college. My grandfather and the boy have little in common, except their connection, in my mind, to the brewery. They lived at different times (Grandpa had died before the boy came to town), but shared this stage.

The young man asked me if he could spend a summer in Akron. He was in love with me, he said. No boy had ever said that to me before, so I told him to buy a bus ticket and come to town. It was the 1960s, and our generation was supposed to be inventing free love. My parents had no comprehension of what this meant, though. They knew there was nothing free about love. Haberkosts were not love children, my mother's eyes told me, but Missouri Synod Lutherans. My parents liked the boy well enough, so didn't mind that he spent the summer here. But I failed to convince them that it would be a good idea for him to stay in our little Tudor house.

So my boyfriend rented a room from an elderly woman who lived across the street from us, and he worked at the Burkhardt Brewery— at least in the buildings the brewery had once occupied. I'm not sure what he did. I may have forgotten to ask. I drove down Grant Street every afternoon to pick my boyfriend up after work. He was always waiting at the top of a ramp, smiling at me, a thin, nervous boy with plump lips that, for a while, I loved to kiss. I loved those lips of his, but never really him.

Uncle Paul called him "Slats" because he was rail thin. He saved the money from all those hot hours and bought a car from another elderly widow on the west side of the city. It was a Ford, I think. Green. It turned out to be what my father called "an oil burner." A lemon before the Lemon Law was legislated. A mean trick by an old woman who preyed on the innocence of boys and cut it right out of them. He drove the car back home when the summer ended. He took me with him (to meet his parents), and the car engine blew up on the highway. We saw steam rising from the hood, then smoke, then fire. Every dollar he had earned in the hot rooms of the old Burkhardt Brewery burned away. I had never been so frightened for the moment, or so aware of my future.

I left the boy two summers after that. I'd stopped enjoying sex with him, and when that was gone, nothing remained. There was no mystery in the dark corners he backed me into anymore. Marriage would have been a contract for our mutual destruction.

Leaving him is one of the deep regrets of my youth. I don't mean that I regret I ended the relationship. That we were mismatched became more and more clear, and our separation was necessary and inevitable. But it's *how* I left that saddens me about myself. I knew so little about his heart when I commanded him *never* to drive three hundred miles to visit me again. *Never* to spend another summer on my street. *Never* to write. *Never* to call. *Never. Never. Never.*

I knew even less about my own heart than I did his. The idea of love hadn't formed there yet. All I was doing all those years when I was with the boy was watching him—trying to learn what he felt for me so that I could feel the same thing one day. *But not for him.* That's the sad center of it all. That was the catch, the thing he may have never suspected. He was patient with me because I think he thought I'd learn to love him if he just waited long enough.

I never did.

I couldn't repay him. Not with love. He deserved a kinder fare-well, a little thanks. A few words that were just his, and no one else's.

So here they are.

I return to my car and proceed to the end of Grant Street, because this is what I have come to do. I don't want to think about the brew-ery anymore.

At the top of the hill close to Exchange, where Uncle Paul's house once stood, the elections office stands. When I get this far, I'm almost out of Goosetown. My uncle's mother, Ludwina Dietrich (everyone called her *Tante Ludy*), had a vegetable garden where Uncle Paul learned how to weed and plant. It's buried under a parking lot. I see some bumps and think they're turnips and potatoes, ready to be picked. I imagine ropes of roots from the American elm my uncle and I stood beside just a few weeks ago.

I laugh as I think that even when Uncle Paul is not sitting in my car, I'm telling his stories for him. He's told them to me so many times that they feel like my own.

I'm ready to head back home. As I turn onto the expressway off Exchange, I know something is beginning to happen, but I'm still not sure it's enough for a book: a brewery, an intersection, a church, Grandpa's white shirt, a little boy named Eddie, a secret shaped like a fish, and a roadbed that rises and dips today exactly as it did long be-fore a single Haberkost arrived.

I don't remember driving on Grant when we lived in Goosetown, but we must have driven the road often—to get the Thanksgiving tur-key, to shop at downtown department stores, to "ooh" and "aah" at Firestone Park, where my father hoped to live one day. I imagine my-self supine in the back seat of our Hudson Hornet, looking through a window at the buildings that rose like chunky, familiar giants.

I feel the roadbed jar my bony spine.

CHAPTER 6

Sometimes you can read history by following a road; sometimes, by tracing the shapes of existing buildings or ones that used to be there. But always, you have to know what's underneath.

Cartography, geometry, geology. That's how you begin to find a place you've lost.

I learned what was under Goosetown from an Akron policeman.

The officer wrote me a letter. He was a friend of my cousin Carol, who works as a dispatcher for the Akron City Police. She had given him my book about Firestone Park, because he liked Akron history. He thought I might be interested in learning more stories about Goosetown. I guess, like my uncle Paul, he noticed that my Goosetown memories were a little thin.

Shortly before the letter arrived, I had visited Jamestown, Virginia, for the first time. I was amazed by the archaeological digs. Students and scientists were discovering what the community had really been like—how James Fort looked and operated, and where the farms and buildings stood in the Virginia Colony—all by slowly and carefully digging with small trowels and moving debris away with brushes. Researchers began with shovels, but quickly moved to smaller instruments. The shovels were too invasive for rooting out the little things, so tiny strokes were used to go a fraction deeper and wider each day. Archaeologists recovered breastplates, skeletons of Jamestown settlers, Indian pots, daggers, musket balls, surgical tools, scissors, a piece of an old abandoned well, a lost ring, a brick church tower (the only structure of the settlement that remains above ground), a silver English halfpenny bearing the Tudor rose and thistle of James I.

I realized, although I'd lived in this country all my life, I had no sense of the European landing of 1607. It really happened, though. I stood on ground adorned with goose shit, as close to the point of arrival of America's first European settlers as anyone can get: the shore has receded by twenty-five feet. I found myself far less interested in recent bronze statues of a busty Pocahontas and an arrogant John Smith than in the artifacts that were lodged in the original ground. I wondered if any remnants of the twenty slaves who were purchased on this shore in 1619 ever would be found, or what those fragments might tell us about their lives.

The story the policeman told also came through excavation.

The letter was about the Burkhardt Brewery. The policeman said that a short while back someone exploring the inside of the old brewery late at night had called the police department to request that an officer be sent out. *For everyone's safety*, the caller had said, *there was something the police needed to see.*

At one time, the old Burkhardt Brewery used an underground stream to make their beer, the officer wrote. Other Akron experts have identified this stream as one source of the beer's distinctiveness. In the early years of Akron history, pure, cool drinking water—fifty-seven degrees on the hottest day of the summer—could easily be found in hidden streams ten, forty, even a hundred feet underground. Burkhardt's Brewery tapped into one of them—the same stream that fed Renner's Brewery across town and Buchtel College for a while—and gathered its waters in holding tanks beneath the floor of the building. But that was a long time ago. Beer hadn't even been manufactured on Grant Street for over forty years.

The man who placed the call had been roaming through the brewery with just a flashlight. He was about to enter a small interior room when he realized the slickness he believed was from some sort of ancient spill was really overflow from an old holding tank.

The tank was full. Even now. After all this time.

The water had filled to the top of the tank and had begun to flood out over the floorboards. *It was twenty feet deep*, he told the officer, *cold and very clear.* It didn't take the officer long to realize that the underground stream was still whirling quietly below. *The old creek is still feeding the brewery after all those years.* I read the last line of the letter again.

The stream is deep, patient, strong, and abiding. Even though people don't use it anymore, and have stopped talking about it, it's still there. As the prowler found out, there's danger in forgetting things that lie hidden below.

The stream is still bubbling up through the ground, effervescent and inexorable. It can't be stopped.

CHAPTER 7

Wherever we travel in Goosetown, Uncle Paul always tries to get me to remember Eagle Street. *You lived on Eagle five years, Babe!* I hear him before we're out of his drive.

It's one of his refrains, like those from patriotic songs he learned in the barbershop chorus he sang in for fifty years. He'd sometimes teach me the lines so I could be ready for the annual show in downtown Akron.

Eagle Street was off Grant, on the south side of Thornton Park. Not a brick or board or square inch of that street remains. But I can see a little of it in my head.

Our house at 208 Eagle Street was skinny and long, like a railroad car. It's odd that most of the houses I've lived in as an adult have looked just like it. There are a few photographs of the street that sharpen things in my memory, and perhaps make memory possible. In addition to the one of me toddling up and down the backyard fence, there are a few of our Pekinese dog, Rusty, several of me sitting on the front steps with cousins and friends, one or two of the people we rented our house from—including their son, the Tin-Can Frisbee Man. It's the outside of the house I remember best, probably because of the photographs.

Evergreen Avenue in Firestone Park is the street I remember clearly. But Uncle Paul has no interest in the Park anymore. He likes

*Uncle Paul backstage holding Stephen Dyer during an Akron
Barbershop Chorus performance in 1975*

to fly his flag and walk his dog there, but Goosetown is the only place
he talks about.

I tell him I remember Eagle Street. It makes him happy to hear me
say that. Once in a while I tell him about the scars from that place.
The one on my forehead, of course, is still there. Several little ones
decorated my knees, but have vanished over the years, so I can't show

him those. Sometimes I think I still see them there or feel them when I touch my legs in the tub, but I know they're gone.

If I want to get the focus off myself, I ask him if he ever saw an eagle on Eagle Street. He laughs, loses his concentration, and lets me off the hook for a while. He always likes a joke.

But I really do wonder what Goosetown looked like long before I arrived. I have no idea if birds that big ever lived here. The Germans brought geese, not eagles, when they came to Akron. I really doubt the immigrants ever saw an eagle in this place.

Still, there were rocky crags in Goosetown that would have made a better home for eagles than the flatter lines today.

I saw a bald eagle flying in the wild once, on Grand Manan Island in New Brunswick, Canada. My husband and I were standing atop dramatic basalt cliffs, and the bird swooped toward us, gliding majestically before turning and flying away. If you can see an eagle, my husband said, he's already seen you for quite a while. I know so little about an eagle's eyes.

Before the geese, in the epoch of eagles, there *were* wolves in Goosetown. Goosetown's official name is Wolf Ledge (even the old Burkhardt Brewery was originally called Wolf Ledge Brewery). Old Washington Street is now named Wolf Ledges Parkway—though I'm pretty sure the wolves were gone even before my grandparents arrived in town in the 1870s and 1880s. Ohio paid the last bounty for a wolf skin in 1842. Thousands of wolves had been poisoned and trapped and hunted, and then one day they were gone. Their hides were on the walls and their bones were in the ground and their stories were in fairy tales about little girls who wandered in the woods looking for Grandma's house.

As boys and girls, my grandparents, perhaps even my uncle Paul, may have found hips, femurs, spines, and snouts and tied them around their arms and necks, like ancient jewelry.

Goosetown, about 1900 (August Herman photo, from C.R. Quine's The Old Wolf Ledge*)*

The huge rocks that made the neighborhood distinct began to disappear when the Loop Line and the Grant Street Line were finished, and streetcars started transporting people from Exchange to South in 1890, fifty years after the wolves vanished. New settlers arrived and a building boom began. At the time, there were only a few houses south of Wheeler to the ledge. Slowly, the ledge was destroyed, fields surveyed, and houses erected. Sumner Street was graded in 1894. The bridge that spanned the gorge was torn down, the gorge was filled in, and Wolf Run was routed under the fill through a stone culvert. Once a picnic spot, Wolf Ledge became a residential community. Wolf Run would be captured and encased in a storm sewer in 1917. The ravine would be completely filled in by 1921. Year by year, Goosetown began to look more like other neighborhoods.

The place had once been a natural wonder. You could dam Wolf Run at various points and swim, climb rocks, explore Old Maid's Kitchen, sit on the enormous steps at its entranceway, walk across Sumner Street bridge and look into the gorge, cross log bridges over steep grades at Allyn, Sherman, Grant, and Washington Streets, pick berries and wildflowers, or gather witch hazel to make home remedies that took away the itch of poison ivy.

The surface of the land had little drama when I lived in Goosetown, but there were still signs of that old rocky place. A huge rock stood across from Grandma's house at the northeast entrance to Thornton Park. Someone once told me it was an actual piece of the original ledge, though I've also heard the story that it was an isolated glacial bit. We loved that rock. I think it presented as much adventure to us as the old ledge and ravine did in Grandpa's day. We had inherited a fondness for rocks from our family's stonemasons. Rock was in our blood, and we couldn't stay away from the one on the corner of Grant and Thornton. There were steps carved into the hill that led up to it—probably meant to discourage people from climbing up the grassy slope and ripping the lawn. We'd run up them to see who could reach the top step first, then mount the stone and ride it. My cousins and I were always racing, testing our legs and speed. Eddie was faster than I was, though Carol, a year older than the two of us, was fastest of all. We were constantly in motion, and our brains and hearts didn't even seem to work yet. We didn't think. We didn't love. We just moved.

When we were young, rock seemed so permanent. Even when the three of us tried to push that rock in Thornton Park—our little palms pressed hard against it and our feet pumping—its resistance was absolute. I think if it had budged a single millimeter our world would have come undone. Perhaps children have always loved rocks because they are stable and they steady us. Earlier generations had seen rock

Annabelle resting against a rocky remnant of old Goosetown, 1920s

everywhere, not just on hills for decoration, as we did. There were sandstone cliffs thirty feet high, completely perpendicular. Sandstone quarries in Goosetown were as common and numerous as mini-marts today. There was one on nearly every corner—Adam Rohner's quarry on Sherman Street, Anthony Hunt's at Allyn, the Henry Zinkand quarry, the Peter Brown quarry, the Wohlwend quarry at Washington Street. I imagine some of the stone for Concordia Lutheran Church came from these quarries, and I know that downtown buildings were made from them.

The rock on the hill is gone now. Long before it disappeared, the quarries were covered up.

But the hardness of Goosetown always remained.

Not much grew on our lot. There's a picture of my mother sitting on the grass trying to punch through the soil with some sharp tool or other to plant seeds. I think I remember the day because it frightened me to see her hit the ground so hard. This was the woman who had never slapped my skin (hardly even touched it). A silent woman, but one who loved the earth in a wild way. Maybe the silence of the ground, its hardness, was the thing that both attracted her and caused her fury.

Nor do I recall any flowers in Grandma's yard. Her house was only one street away, and her soil was just as barren as ours. I've seen photos that prove it. Dirt and grass press right up to the stone foundation. Bushes mark the property line on either side, but they are stark, without a blossom ever visible. There had been a tree in the front yard when my mother was young (I've seen it in a photograph), but it was gone by my time. I don't associate flowers with my grandmother. The only flowers I think of when I remember my mother came into her life after we moved to Firestone Park: the lilacs and lilies of the valley on her table; a single blossom of purple clematis from the arbor that arched over our door, floating in a bowl.

Annabelle in front of the Grant Street house when there had been a tree

My uncle often repeats that the absence of trees on Princeton Street in Goosetown was why he moved.

Although the move never altered his affection for Goosetown, Uncle Paul loved his new backyard on Ivy Place. He began to grow rhubarb and flowers (bleeding hearts, hosta, coreopsis, daffodils, tulips, geraniums), and to worship Mrs. Lovingood. There were no wiser seers in his life than people who gave him garden tips, and she was one of them. Mrs. Lovingood lived one street south, and her backyard butted up against my uncle's. She frequently came over to see what was growing in his garden, and he did the same. She was, according to him, the best gardener in Akron. We didn't appreciate her then, of course. Her backyard garden seemed to be the only thing she cared about (along with George, her husband), and we were prohibited from cutting through it after school to get to my uncle's house. She hated kids, we thought, and yelled at us if we harmed her plants, so we decided to hate her too. It seemed only fair. What kind of person would like squash and honeysuckle more than kids? But Uncle Paul always defended her. *She's quite a woman. Taught me how to braid daffodils at the end of the summer.* He'd go on to explain how braiding nourished next season's bulbs, and we knew he was asking us to be kind to Mrs. Lovingood.

It was at the Ivy Place house that my uncle began his ritual of sitting on a pillow and pulling dandelions. We'd often sit beside him, and he'd show us how to pry the roots loose. When he weeded in the front, he greeted everyone who said hello to him—the milkman, the pregnant teenager one door down that no one else talked to, the neighbor's pet crow that landed on his steps. Uncle Paul didn't follow us around all the time the way some adults did (the veins in his legs always gave him trouble, and he didn't move as quickly as other men), but he was always in the distance, and you knew where to find him if you needed to. He was our sitting Buddha.

One of the first things Uncle Paul did when he moved was plant raspberries next to his garage. Even with little light, the plants grew. They never flourished, but a few berries always ripened. We didn't eat them, though, at least not while Grandma was alive. They were *hers*. Year after year, when fruit ripened, Uncle Paul would announce that the berries were ready for Grandma Haberkost. He would pick them just for her, and take them to the Grant Street house. Uncle Paul talks about the berries whenever we drive by the site where the house once stood.

Carol, Paul, and author in the backyard of Uncle Paul's house on Ivy Place

After both families left Goosetown (they moved to Firestone Park on the same day), my parents seemed genuinely glad to get away and seldom returned, except to visit Grandma and attend the Lutheran church on Sumner and Voris. I loved our new house, and my cousin lived nearby, so I didn't miss Goosetown any more than my parents did. My father loved his new life in Firestone Park as much as he had thought he would, so Tom Coyne never wanted to stay long when we drove to Goosetown to visit my mother's mother. I could feel it in the big sighs he took and the way he squirmed in Grandma's narrow chairs (so unlike the stuffed couch he rested on in our new living room). We were on our way up, and that old place was on its way out. Returning to Grant Street made my mother sad, too. Not for the reasons it made my ambitious father sad, but for reasons of her own that she never shared with us.

Grandma died in 1959 and my father sold her house. After that, the name *Goosetown* was rarely spoken and its story ended for the Coynes. Little remained to remind us of it anymore. All that was left from Anna Haberkost's estate were a few dollars (her life savings was $944.02, and upon her death she received a refund of $5.94 from her fire insurance policy), a couple of pieces of glass and stemware, one housedress that she had never worn, and a small lithograph that had hung in my grandparents' living room. My mother stored it in the corner of a portable metal clothes closet, and then it passed to me.

There's a picture of the front face of the Eagle Street house. It's dated July 20, 1950, my third birthday. I'm sitting with nine friends on the steps that lead up to the porch. Something was wrong, but I have no memory of what. My cousin Paul is beside me, his hand in a small bag of popcorn, and poor Eddie is on the step below me, holding his bag tightly closed. The girls have bows and barrettes in their hair, and their hands are folded in their laps. But my hands are pressed to the sides of my face, and my fingers seem to be holding in my brain. My face is scrunched. I look like the figure in Edvard Munch's *The Scream*. I don't know what was wrong with me when the camera flashed, but sometimes I feel as if my hands are still in that position, my head about to pop.

CHAPTER 8

"You have Travelin' Pie?"

Uncle Paul and I are in a restaurant in Firestone Park, having lunch again, getting ready to set off on another wild goose chase.

Our server has no idea what my uncle is talking about. She just stands by our table and stares at him, her upper lip lifted a little too high for a smile.

I laugh and double over.

I've become my uncle's translator, his straight man. After I recover from his joke, I tell her he wants to place a take-out order for dessert. He's so tickled by what he's said—and the confusion of the server— that he turns his mouth to the side and holds a cotton handkerchief over his nose, as if he's blowing it. Then I see his shoulders shake.

You'd think he was a boy of fifteen, not an old man of eighty-nine.

"Sure," she says. "What kind you want?"

"You have rhubarb?" (He must be thinking about his old garden.)

"No."

"Gooseberry?"

"Don't have that."

"*Goosetown* just down the street from us, and you don't have gooseberry?"

"Sorry."

"How 'bout cake? You have pineapple upside down?"

The server yells back to the kitchen and finds out they still have a slice or two. I can't believe that Steinly's Restaurant has homemade upside down cake on their lunch menu.

It was a popular cake when I was growing up in South Akron—Steinly's is about as South Akron as a restaurant gets—but it's not a dessert you see very often these days. Even in diners, it's pretty rare. I think of my mother opening a can of pineapple in our home on Evergreen Avenue in Firestone Park for those special occasions when she'd decorate a round yellow cake made from a Betty Crocker mix with rings of fruit, dots of maraschino cherries, and brown sugar so thick it looked like sand.

I learned how to cook from my aunt Ruth (when I had sense enough to watch) and, later, from my brother-in-law.

"Your name Hilda?" Uncle Paul asks after the cake arrives. The letters of Darlene's name are displayed in silver glitter on her nametag, an inch high.

"Darlene," she says, pointing.

"Geraldine?"

"*Dar*lene."

"*Darling*? Gosh, that's nice." He looks at me. "This here's *Babe*," he says to her. "I think the two of you should meet."

Uncle Paul has crazy names for everyone and everything. Half the time you don't know what he's talking about. His son, Paul, is "Pinky" (*Born real pink!* he told everyone for years, until his son became a physician and politely asked him to stop), my cousin Carol is "Laup" ("*Paul*" *spelled backwards*, he says), and I'm "Babe"—the name he chose because I was born after the others were, younger by just a year or two. He called Eddie "Howard," which was Eddie's middle name, as well as the name of August and Anna's first-born son. I just barely remember that.

Author, Carol, and Paul Jr. with Anna Haberkost

Paul, Carol, and I were always more like siblings than first cousins. Paul Jr. was an only child, and so was I. Carol had two brothers,
but one of them, Jimmy, was from her mother's first marriage, so he
was several years older. He wasn't exactly Carol's stepbrother, though.
Marie, her mother, married her first husband twice. It took me a long
time to process that. The second union produced Carol and her
brother Eddie. All three children were products of the same parents,
but different marriages. When Eddie died, Carol pretty much became
an only child, too. Just like me. And just like Paul. Early photographs
often show the three of us together, performing in Jean Shepherd

dance recitals at the Akron Armory, playing school, sitting with Grandma on a tired piece of furniture somewhere.

I drive Uncle Paul under the Princeton Street bridge after we leave Steinly's Restaurant with the cake. Princeton Street is where he's asked to go today. He misses Ruth and the street where they lived as newlyweds. He *always* misses Ruth.

Living on a street with a name like "Princeton" was the closest most people in my uncle's generation ever got to the Ivy League. Other small streets parallel to Princeton had equally improbable names— Yale, Bowdoin, Harvard, Amherst. The hard-working men and women of Goosetown who grew up in the Depression seldom attended college. It was a dream they had for their children, not for themselves.

You can drive down Thornton Street to reach the Princeton Street bridge, but today Uncle Paul insists that I take him on the expressway so he can show me where his house was from down below.

"Duck!" he shouts as we drive underneath the bridge. "Quack! Quack!"

I laugh and lower my head a little. He's startled me. I should be used to his tricks by now.

"Did you see it?" he says. "We just drove through my cellar, Babe."

We exit the expressway and climb back toward the old streets of Akron, finally turning onto Princeton and then driving *over* the bridge. Uncle Paul lived at 893 Princeton. I notice the numbers on the houses that remain, and smile when I realize his cellar *would* have been exactly where he said.

He points to a building that appears just south of the bridge. I look at it, but my eye moves quickly to a larger structure off to the right, sitting on a hill. It's Lincoln School, where I attended kindergarten for just two months before we moved to Firestone Park. I try to

Author and her mother in front of Lincoln School

recall my teacher's name, but I can't. I can't remember a single thing that happened once I opened the school's great doors and disappeared inside. I remember the heavy doors and the steps, but little else. It has become another granite shape. I remember my kindergarten teacher, Mrs. Kirk, at Firestone Park Elementary School, but have no idea who my teacher was in this other place. In an old family scrapbook, there's a picture of me holding my mother's hand, standing on the broad stone steps of Lincoln School. My father must have taken it, or Aunt Ruth. Tom Coyne, my dad, started work at 8:00 (*on the dot, Honey!*), so it was probably Ruth who was the photographer. I seldom remember her not being with us. I seldom remember being alone with my mother.

Maybe it's the first day of class. In the old black and white, I'm standing sideways, my right leg bent awkwardly to reach the step above. My mother and I are holding hands, my left in her right. She's smiling, dressed in a two-piece black suit and simple black hat—ready for work at the Akron Board of Education. A rhinestone button secures a veil to the hat and glistens in the bright sun. I'm wearing a light cotton skirt, though you can't see much of it because my mother has draped me in a dark cape. I'm sure she sewed every piece of clothing we had on. My blond hair looks as white as the building's limestone, though it's no more substantial than the down of a little chick, and I'm squinting so hard that my pupils have vanished into folds of bird skin. My legs are as thin as an egret's.

"A grocer and a butcher shared the space," Uncle Paul tells me, shifting my focus back to the old store in front of us. "Divided the building right in half. Names were Irwin Lawbaugh and Carl Morgan."

He shakes his head and smiles. "Funny I can remember a thing like that but I can't remember what I had for lunch. What *did* I have for lunch, Babe?" I hold up his Steinly's bag and shake it gently, and he smiles. "Travelin' Pie," I say.

We drive back down Grant and into his driveway.

Travelin' Pie in hand, he slowly climbs the four steps to his back door, turns his key, and twists the knob. I hear birdsong spill from his door alert, and know he's safely in the house, so I close the sunroof of my car and drive away. I imagine him inside, eating pie.

CHAPTER 9

Uncle Paul looks for ghosts on our drives, and I've begun to look for them too. They're harder to find than the buildings and the roads, but not impossible.

He looks for Ruth everywhere—on Princeton Street, in Thornton Park. There's nothing left of Thornton Park, of course. It doesn't matter. We pull into the parking lot of the post office and he finds her.

This is where they meet.

He stands outside the car for a few minutes, and they have a rendezvous.

I can see him shake his head and hear him mutter "Poor Ruth!" through the open window. He's thinking about his wife's cancer that was diagnosed too late. The only thing they could do was remove her breast and radiate the lymph nodes in the area. Chemotherapy was still experimental, so they didn't try. By the time they cut the breast away, cancer had spread through her body. Before a year was out, it would take a lung and twist her spine. She'd be wearing a painful brace across her back, and each morning Uncle Paul would lace it up, and tie it in a bow.

They gave her morphine around the clock. Uncle Paul quit his job the day he was told there was no hope for his wife, and retired without his full pension. Aunt Ruth had just turned sixty. Uncle Paul

Ruth Steurer as a young woman

has lived nearly thirty years since Ruth's been gone on his small pension. Meals on Wheels brings him lunch. He has few luxuries. But I've heard him voice only one regret.

"I wasn't in the room when she died," he often says, shaking his head. He wanted most of all to be with her when she died. That's why he quit his job. He wanted her to look over and see him smiling at her, and feel his fingers all tangled in hers. It was his last wish, but it wasn't granted.

I always remember Ruth and Paul tangled up in each other. He would walk through his house with his arm around Ruth's waist, and she'd fuss with his collar or the cuffs on his shirt. Oh, the lovely Ruth, her small frame, her perfect legs, her sweet heart. He thanked her for every meal—for everything she did for him—and made her laugh by nibbling on her cheek, pretending to devour her, or lowering his glasses and looking straight into her eyes with such fierce affection that when I first saw it as a child I had no idea what it was. Later, respectful of the moment, I would turn away.

I also remember tension between them. She would slam the door and walk out of the house. Uncle Paul would pace until she returned, and we wouldn't talk to him because we felt he wasn't even there. He would tease her too much, laugh at her scolding tongue. Her love had a sharp edge to it, and sometimes Uncle Paul would try to soften it. But that edge, which made her voice a little too shrill, was the thing that let her love cut into people and find a place inside to stay attached. We all knew it, too, but sometimes we forgot. She'd slam the door, but always come back before long.

Omissions lurk everywhere in my uncle's world. Sitting in the post office parking lot, I see him stare at a woman he loves who isn't even there. Driving under a bridge, he takes me on a tour of a cellar that's been gone for fifty years. Our trips are becoming more and more spectral, and I wonder if anyone can even see us as we pass.

He's paid his respects, and now he moves to the courtship scene. I see the lines of his face soften and dissolve. He likes to play his life in reverse, ending with the early years. This spot where the parking lot stands is where they met. I don't think Thornton Park had a swimming pool when he was young. It was there in the 1950s when I was a kid, but all my uncle talks about are the swings and the baseball field, so if the pool was there, he doesn't remember it. But why would he have noticed the pool, when there was Ruth? When there's a mermaid, no one sees the water.

He first noticed her on a creaky swing after a ballgame. He's told me the story many times. His team had won the game, and he was singing and whistling his way out of the park. There she was in front of him, pumping with all the energy in her strong legs, back straight and perfect, her billowing skirt catching him like a sail and changing his direction forever. I imagine my uncle with his fielder's mitt in his nervous hand, Ruth's brown curls spilling everywhere. I hear her giggle at the first joke he will ever tell her, and watch her begin to fall in love.

And then my memory picks up the story. I see them living in Firestone Park, my uncle sitting on his famous pillow in the grass, Ruth hanging clothes behind him on a line of rope. I see her small sturdy hips sway with the rope as she removes a wooden clothespin from her mouth, bends to take a shirt from the basket at her side, then catches line and cloth and wind and secures them all. I see myself turning awkward cartwheels between the two of them, sometimes hitting a skirt or towel with my heel. *Be careful, young lady!* she screams at me, but I'm not afraid. The intricacy and grace of my aunt's every movement as she walks up and down the line—so apparent next to my clumsy flips—must have been visible to my uncle Paul. The way she bent and lifted herself, the elegant way her fingers danced along the rope line, the tiny steps she took down the row as she hung a shirt. My uncle must have wanted to touch her all the time.

Now Uncle Paul begins to hum. But I don't know where the sound is coming from. Is he beside me in the passenger seat, an old man? Or in the backyard where Ruth is pinning clothes? There's humming everywhere, old vocal chords mixing with the sound of honeybees.

It soon turns into his favorite German song—"Du, Du Liegst Mir im Herzen."

What's that mean? I, the child in the scene, will ask him, half-listening as I stare at the stains on my palms and the sun spinning above my head.

You, you, place me in your heart, he will say, and glance at Ruth.

Oh, I will say.

The next cartwheel will already be forming in my mind. I will quickly forget my aunt and uncle and raise my arms straight and high in the air, like the metal hands on a clock at noon. I will forget his answer to my question.

But when I'm much older, I'll ask again.

"What's that mean?" I say as we head down Grant, toward home.

This time, I remember his reply.

CHAPTER 10

I'm able to read my uncle better than I used to.

There are things I've missed because I haven't always understood old men, but slowly I'm learning my uncle's refrains.

There's his line about the ovary, for instance. Uncle Paul often tells me my mother had just one ovary. Usually after he says that, there's a pause. Then, he gets his breath and launches into the story of my babyhood.

Good gravy Grandmother, he always says. *You never stopped yellin'*!

But before he tells me how much I cried, he recites the line about my mother's ovary.

On a postcard he sent just a few weeks ago—with a picture on the front of a place he hadn't been to (he collects postcards from all over the world and then mails them from Akron)—he greeted me (of course) with the refrain about the ovary. *Did I ever tell you that your mother had just one ovary?* He was thinking about my mother, and when he thinks about her, he thinks about her ovary. Even Annabelle never told me about it. Not once. It was always Uncle Paul. She had had a cyst that led to the only operation of her long life, and the removal of an ovary.

He then explained on the card how things were after I was born, which is what he always does after he mentions the ovary.

You were too much for your mom, he wrote. *Babe, you nearly drove her nuts.*

I think the absence of the ovary, in his mind, helps him understand why I was *too much* for my mother. It explains something important. Something he needs to understand. The absence of that ovary, my uncle reasons, somehow diminished Annabelle, made her less maternal, less patient with children than other women were. My mother wasn't fond of babies, so, in his typically generous manner, Uncle Paul looks for a way to excuse her.

Perhaps a way that *I* might excuse her, too.

The missing ovary is the best that he can do, even though there isn't any science to it.

He seldom blames people for anything. Defending them, he'll sometimes make excuses. At my father's funeral, Uncle Paul delivered a short eulogy, and told a whopper about my dad that I still haven't forgotten.

Tom Coyne, he mused, *never said an unkind word about anyone.* And then he said it again. Just about the same way. *Never judged, never criticized.*

Who was he talking about? I wondered. I loved Tom Coyne fiercely. I don't know how he could possibly have been a better father to me than he was. But *uncritical* of other people?

My father screamed at auto mechanics (except for Leffler and Glenn), insulted the grocer at the Acme store, once accused an elementary school teacher of theft, said terrible things about some of my mother's sisters, and made servers take overcooked meat or lumpy mashed potatoes back to the kitchen. I had heard him on more than one occasion yell out our window at an eccentric neighbor lady. Especially late in his career at Firestone, he was angry a lot of the time and easily took offense. He wasn't mean (certainly never to me), but he was hard on people he felt had done him wrong. On the day of the funeral for my dad, Paul Steurer saw only St. Thomas.

Paul Jr. and author dressed as cowboy twins

Uncle Paul often mentions that Aunt Ruth and he *adopted* me. He says it lightly, in the teasing way he has. They wanted two children, he says—*wanted a girl real bad*—and I was available. He assures me I didn't give them any trouble. In photographs I frequently see his son and me dressed as twins, with matching cowboy shirts and cowboy hats, matching Halloween outfits, matching costumes for tap dancing recitals. My mother would sew the outfits while my aunt Ruth was taking care of us. Paul Jr. was small, even though he was two years older than I was, so for a long time, no one questioned this strange fabrication. During my first pre-pubescent growth spurt, however, I left my "twin" behind by an entire head.

Uncle Paul tells me that whenever the screaming wouldn't stop, my mother dropped me off at Grandma's house, or Ruth's.

But the image of the colicky baby is far less interesting to me than the shadow of Annabelle Haberkost Coyne as she tries to step into the role of motherhood, a role she'd never studied, never practiced, never learned.

I remember her in Firestone Park, and throughout my adult life, as extremely calm and capable. This was not the same person from the Goosetown years, according to my uncle Paul, so I've begun to look for her.

There's not a folder neatly labeled "Annabelle's Early Mother-hood—the Difficult Goosetown Years." But in stray, dusty corners there are small signs of my mother's deep unhappiness with her ma-ternal role. I've located details that help fill in my uncle's story of the *colicky baby* and the *ovary*, and, of course, of the *adoption* that brought peace to the family again.

I've found a copy of a birth announcement, the one my grandpa Coyne received. It was in my baby book—which has only about four pages filled; the rest are blank. My mother quickly tired of it, it seems.

The announcement isn't typed (my mother would have used her Royal upright), nor is it written in my father's hand. It's Uncle Paul's script. It's odd that neither my mother *nor* my father sent the an-nouncements. Even if my mother was too upset to fill them out, why wouldn't my dad have written them? No one had more pride in family than he did. And few in our family were as loquacious as Tom Coyne.

I look at the tiny card with a sweet little baby on it, a happy baby in pink booties, holding a blue rabbit ("A Star Is Born," it reads on the front).

The beginning of the lasting friendship of Paul, Ruth, Annabelle, and Tom

Everything is filled in, name, birthdate, weight, parents' names, but by my uncle Paul. A few fun-loving phrases are added afterwards:

"You can't tell a player without a score card."

"Time she started to take after her father and cry: 12:32 in the afternoon."

"Any more information call Pinky's father."

"P.S. Please don't reverse the charges."

Uncle Paul is being his usual silly self, but why was he stepping in? Annabelle and Tom had waited eleven years to have a child. The only explanation I can imagine is that whatever was happening to my mother was unbearable. It—I!—had taken energy and will, desire and hope right out of Annabelle, and then she pried them out of Tom. Tom Coyne could not even send an announcement to his own father about the birth of a healthy baby girl.

I see my uncle standing in the Eagle Street house, feeling tension between Annabelle and Tom for the first time in the many years he's known them. A baby cries, and then its mother sobs. Tom is trying to comfort both a daughter and a wife, but he doesn't know how to do either. His knees are shaking, and his nerves are as dangerous as open wires. Uncle Paul feels helpless. He notices the neglected stack of announcements on my mother's typing table, stuffs them in his pocket, and fills them out at his mahogany desk when he returns home. He doesn't remember doing this when I ask. The entire episode has been replaced with the image of a colicky baby and a lonely ovary.

There's a second scrap to examine—not in my baby book, but in another folder of my mother's labeled "Akron Board of Education." It's an official letter to the Board Office, typed by my mother just weeks after I was born. It would result in her returning to work. "I have made a terrible mistake," it begins.

My mother formally resigned before I was born, quitting her job forever, the way other women did at the time. She declared her profession as "HW," housewife, on my birth certificate. But unlike others who resigned, she sent a letter to her employer asking to come back. She had *made a terrible mistake*. What did she think the mistake was, though? Was it just leaving her position? Was it letting love swell into a pregnancy? Was it discovering too quickly that she did not like infants and had no talent for handling them? Was it realizing how much she would miss her adding machine and smoking in the coffee room with her friends?

Was it finding out, even after a few days, that she would rather work than raise a daughter?

Doctors had no idea what to do to help a woman like Annabelle in 1947. I'm not sure they do now. Motherhood was not the right choice for her. She found no joy in it. It didn't feel *natural*, the way I'm sure all her friends had told her that it would.

Annabelle at her desk at the Akron Board of Education

I *wonder*, as I think of her now—
Where does maternity originate?
Could she have found any way to be happy in this new role?
Is the kind of deep affection and selflessness that motherhood requires woven in our DNA?

I sensed in Annabelle the same coolness toward children that my grandma Haberkost always had. I have no recollection of my mother touching me during the Goosetown years (except the day my parents swooped me up after the tin can sailed off course). Even after we moved to the Park, Annabelle never grabbed me or kissed me hard. She seldom ever did more than hold my hand or peck a cheek.

Anna, my grandma, my mother's namesake, was like that too. With her grandkids she was always cool, the way her daughter was with me.

I don't know whether Anna Haberkost liked having as many children as she did. She bore seven over a period of sixteen years. She dressed and cared for them all pretty much alone. She was forty-two when her last child, Betty, arrived. Not much older than my own mother when she had me, her first, and only, child. I can't say whether Anna Haberkost really loved the physical pleasure of holding a newborn and swaddling it in her arms every two years.

I cannot speak for her. But I have a picture of her with me as an infant that makes me think she didn't want the life that both the man she married and her biology had given her. I was three months old in the photograph. It's October 1947. Grandma is sitting in a chair in her backyard, holding me. I guess that's what you'd call it. I can feel her bones as I look at it. They almost poke through the paper. Her fingers are spread out over my blanket, like spider legs, and I've sunk deep into her lap. I'm as far away from her cheek as a baby can get. She doesn't touch me with her hands. Her body is as straight and sharp-edged as the chimney behind her in the sky. Not a single cell of her bends toward me. Her head stares straight into the camera, no suggestion of a smile anywhere on her face. Her legs are an old woman's legs, brittle and bowed, and it looks as if they might collapse at any time, and I'll be lost. If I fall, my neck will snap, and someone will come with a dust pan and sweep me up, along with Grandma's bones, and take us to a charnel house.

My grandma had petrified by the time I was born. If the picture had not been taken, I would have forgotten her skin. A child needs flesh to sink into, not bone.

Perhaps my mother was the fleshless kind, like Anna Haberkost, her mother. Perhaps Annabelle was made of mostly bone, and there wasn't a single thing she could do about it. Or maybe she was just very, very afraid. Maybe she had seen what having children had done to her own mother, and she knew she had to run away when she saw

Grandmother Haberkost holding author in the backyard of 624 Grant Street

me screaming in my crib. She couldn't allow what happened to Anna
to happen to her. Or perhaps she was in love with the Akron Board of
Education and refused to give it up for anyone or anything. In some
way, was she sensing what was on the horizon for her—Alzheimer's?
Did her genes know that one of them would take her mind and stub-
bornly insist she use her brain while it lived?

But I think now that my mother's decision is tied inextricably to the story of Ruth and Paul adopting me. Especially, to the story of Ruth.

I'm not entirely sure my mother would have written that letter begging to return to work without Ruth, her sister. She wouldn't have abandoned me, no matter how sad I made her. Or would she have? I know that other good women have left their young, so maybe she *would* have walked away. A part of me wants her to stay and a part of me wants her to run away as quickly as she can.

I witnessed her fury and rebellion on only one occasion: when she started down the long road of Alzheimer's. It was a mighty thing. It took me by surprise and made me think a demon was in Annabelle. She struck me with her hard fist, and refused to obey me or anyone. I think that demon came out whenever fate turned against her, so it might also have appeared in Goosetown, when a smiling nurse placed a colicky baby in her arms for the first time. I think that's how demons are born—in moments of surprise.

Even if there had been no Aunt Ruth, and Annabelle had remained the dutiful wife and mother she was never cut out to be, a part of her would still have fled forever the day she realized that the joy I gave would be canceled by the joy I took away.

But Ruth *was* there, and she set my mother free.

CHAPTER 11

Ruth was my mother's salvation.

I'm sure it was Ruth who laid the plan and made the offer.

During the Goosetown years, my mother would drop me off at Aunt Ruth's house on her way to work in the morning. I have vague memories of this. Annabelle or Tom would pick me up in late afternoon and take me back to Eagle Street. After we moved to the Park, this pattern continued, except that now I'd stay even longer, often into supper and sometimes later still. Aunt Ruth would give me my bath, and then my father would come for me, or Uncle Paul would walk me home. Sometimes I'd stay at the Steurers' house all night.

Aunt Ruth did my mother's wash and ironing, and cared for Annabelle's daughter. She cleaned our house every single day, walking from Ivy Place to Evergreen Avenue at the top of a steep hill in all weather. Ruth never drove. Even if she had been able to, the Steurers couldn't afford a second car, and Uncle Paul took the Ford every day to the Goodrich Tire & Rubber Company. Ruth carried a straw wash basket between her arms as she climbed the hill to our house. She made our beds every morning and my mother paid her on Friday nights when Uncle Paul drove her to our house with the basket, full of perfectly folded clothes, in the back seat of his car. Aunt Ruth joined the PTA and brought cookies to my class, just after she delivered them to her son's. One year she was her son's room mother, and the

Author with Paul Jr. and the boys of Princeton Street

next year she was mine. When my parents would take vacations alone, I'd stay with Grandma or with Ruth and Paul. The Steurers never seemed to go anywhere, or need to leave town to be happy, the way my parents did.

On Evergreen Avenue, I played with other little girls. Over at the Steurers', on Princeton Street and Ivy Place, I played with boys. There, I learned to build model airplanes from balsa wood kits, to assemble plastic ships with slippery decals, to play basketball and four square, to throw rocks at cars when Uncle Paul wasn't looking, to like cowboy stars (especially Roy Rogers and Dale Evans, and Penny on *Sky King*, whose father owned a plane), to pretend that Paul Jr.'s friends were all in love with me, to read Zane Grey, to give my dolls boys' names (*Roger* was my favorite), to identify dinosaurs (which the

Ruth Steurer and author

pastor at Concordia Lutheran Church insisted never had lived and would ruin our souls if we believed in them), to collect stamps, and to name the bones in the plastic toy skeleton my cousin unwrapped one Christmas when he was very young (perhaps the first step in his progression toward becoming the Bone Man).

I never preferred Ruth to Annabelle, or Annabelle to Ruth. They were equally important to me. They were two halves of a single thing. Aunt Ruth took me to buy a training bra, and explained menstruation and boys to me while we baked cookies and decorated them with butter cream icing. My mother taught me to sew and showed me what my hands could do. Aunt Ruth helped me care for my parakeets, gossiped with me, and made me laugh. Annabelle sat quietly on the sofa (when my father was away) reading a James Hilton novel that had just arrived from the Reader's Digest Condensed Book Club, asked me to sit beside her, and told me I could read about Shangri-La one day. Ruth taught me to fill empty bottles with colored water and place them on a windowsill, and Annabelle showed me how to win at bridge. Ruth took me on the bus to eat potato soup downtown at the Colonial Restaurant before dancing school. My mother drove me to her office and let me write on her typewriter while she spilled yards and yards of paper from her adding machine onto the floor. Ruth waited for Paul to take her everywhere. Annabelle loved owning her own car and loved best the drives she took alone.

When Ruth died, my mother lost her favorite sister, as well as all the things she knew she lacked. Ruth died too soon, but if she had died any sooner, before we were grown, the family may have collapsed without her. After the service for her at Schermesser's Funeral Home, her son, who had tried so hard to keep grief in during the long days of her illness, uttered a sound I had never heard before, and have never heard since. He was "the doctor," after all, who'd remained clinical and scientific about the cancer metastasizing in his mother's bones, bones he could not fix, no matter how fine his education had been (Ruth worked at a shoe store to help pay for it). But in the funeral home, all of his despair broke loose into a single gush of sound. I'm still not sure I can describe it. It was a scream, but it was backwards, formed from a huge sucking in of hollow wind. There was an echo, and it wouldn't stop, as if broad wings of horrible birds were flapping in his mouth, looking for the body of his mother, because he had just devoured her. It was a sound that didn't belong anywhere. But it was there, in that room, and I want to understand it.

I wish I could summon the ghost of Ruth.

Ruth chose to spend her time on earth keeping my mother's house and her daughter clean as a whistle (*Brusha . . .Brusha . . .Brusha.*

Ruth and Annabelle in Goosetown

*New Ipana Toothpaste! Twenty Mule Team Borax. The Good House-
keeping Seal of Approval*). Chose to spend it worrying about our cuts
and scrapes. *That looks angry*, she'd always say when we'd come crying to her with skinned elbows and knees. She'd daub on mercuro-
chrome, and then wince, taking air into her mouth through her teeth,
as if she could suck the pain right out of our bodies and into her own.

If I could sit with her now on a Friday evening, we'd go through
the items in that wash basket she carried to our house. I would notice
the creases in the handkerchiefs, the flatness of the fabric around every button and buttonhole, the deep aroma of bleach and morning
air, the way delicate straps on bras and slips had been smoothed by
her thumbnails and careful eyes. I'd pick the whole basket up and feel
the weight of all those trips down Ruth's basement stairs to the wring-

er washer, then up again with the wet clothes and out the door to the clothesline, and the lifting of cloth and the pinning and then the un-pinning and the lifting of fabric again, the pressing of fingers and palms on stubborn straps and bands, the weight of the iron and the heat of a kitchen in summertime, and the endless worry about stains and missing buttons and frayed collars and all the rest of it. I'd stare at her and be unable to thank her or know what to say, so I'd unbutton her blouse, unzip her skirt, help her slip out of everything, and begin to wash for her. I'd scrub her clothes on a board until my knuckles were raw. I would continue until I fell asleep, and then I'd start again. I'd wash and clean until I'd paid the debt I owed to her. And then I'd scrub harder, deeper, because I'd understand I could never do enough.

And, soon, I would realize that this was my profession. It was what I would do. It would take living in gratitude for the rest of my life to pay for this. Ruth was the woman who held me when I screamed, who held my sick son when he screamed, and who, I know, would have given anything to have climbed out of her own casket at Schermess-er's Funeral Home to comfort her own son the day he screamed his discovery that love and despair are one.

CHAPTER 12

One morning at breakfast, I pull the Quaker Oats box off the shelf, pry off the top, and smell Goosetown.

How could I have forgotten the smell of oats?

The odor from the box is as strong as a field of grain. My nose moves closer and closer to flakes housed in a container shaped like a grain silo and made famous by the funny, pudgy Quaker man on the front with rosy cheeks and a smiling face. Every morning in Goosetown, that smell came in my window and woke me up. All of Goosetown—and much of Akron—smelled like Quaker Oats. I don't remember eating Quaker Oats back then, but we didn't need to. The odor was as thick as the cereal itself. I breathed a bowlful every day.

Rubber and oats were always in south Akron's air, but in Goosetown oats won out.

I call my uncle Paul and tell him to finish his cornflakes because I'm coming down.

I want to find out what he remembers about oats. The house where he grew up was even closer to the mills than ours. We lived four long blocks south of Uncle Paul's family home, four blocks farther from the mills.

He wants to eat at the Waterloo Restaurant first, he tells me, so that's what we'll do. It's a little early, but there's always onion soup in the kitchen at the Waterloo.

We drive down Firestone Boulevard, turn left on South Main, and head toward Waterloo Road. When he sees the Firestone Memorial, with the bronze statue of Harvey S. Firestone and a giant field of wild-flowers in front, he salutes and says, "Hi, Harve!"

I look over at him and snicker.

"I always talk to him when I go by," he tells me. "Must get a little lonely sitting on that hill day after day by yourself." I know what he's thinking, though he covers things up with jokes all the time. He's thinking how lonely it is living with just Edith's dog. A few years after Ruth died, he married Ruth's friend Edith from the shoe store and moved into her house on the 1300th block of Grant Street. Her dog, a golden retriever named Ginger, outlived Edith, so Uncle Paul has only that dog now and no wife. Ruth and Edith are both gone. He sometimes writes me letters about how lonely he is, saying over and over that he wishes the dog could talk, not just eat the canned green beans he buys her at the grocery store.

When I was in high school, the Waterloo on Waterloo Road was the drive-in everyone went to on Friday nights, so I don't mind coming here, for old time's sake. Before I was old enough to drive, my family brought me. The restaurant burned down in 1960, but quickly rose again. In the early days there were always Soap Box Derby specials—a hamburger, milkshake, and pie for sixty-nine cents. For years Uncle Paul volunteered to work Topside at the Derby, for Goodrich, helping to check tires on racers and fraternizing with Derby celebrities. He's told me that's where he made friends with Roy Rogers, Dinah Shore, and Don Ameche. He remembers Dinah Shore singing for three hours straight in a rain delay. Sometimes he still wears his Derby pins on the collars of his shirts, right next to his American flag.

We all loved the Derby specials at the Waterloo, but the menu was *always* good. Apple dumplings with a crust and ice cream on top

Quaker Oats Company, 1940s (Courtesy Summit County Historical Society, Akron, Ohio)

called "Big Apples" have been popular for five decades. You can't get foot-long fish burgers anymore, though it's probably just as well.

The Waterloo looks different inside now. In the corners of the room, electric signs with dancing messages thank customers for their patronage and Christian knick-knacks are on display tables in the lobby. Several customers wear large gold crosses around their necks.

After we finish our onion soup, wedges of cornbread, and Big Apples, Uncle Paul and I move toward the cash register to pay.

We push the turquoise door of the restaurant open and leave.

"Krispy Kreme, anyone?" I ask.

"Sure!" says Uncle Paul, never able to turn down a Krispy Kreme.

Krispy Kremes are the doughnuts I grew up on. They're probably in my veins and arteries now, floating like the little hot dogs and slices of cake you see on posters at CVS Pharmacy by the blood pressure machine. When Rita Dove came to speak at the school where I teach, I had a dozen ready for her, because she's an Akron girl. There's no better way to make a former Akronite feel at home than to serve them a dozen Krispy Kremes. There's a Krispy Kreme on the corner of Waterloo and South Main, just catty-corner from Holy Cross Cemetery, where my parents rest. When I was a kid, there was only one Krispy Kreme, and it was across town, close to Perkins Park and the zoo, on Maple Street. In the 1950s, the Akron Zoo was basically a children's zoo with ducks and pigs and rabbits running around in scenes from Mother Goose rhymes. Imagine how we felt when Aunt Ruth took us with her on the city bus for an afternoon at the Akron Zoo and then a trip to Krispy Kreme. I stay away from cholesterol these days, so I can't have them anymore. But I really don't have any regrets. They wouldn't taste as good without a trip to the old zoo with my aunt Ruth.

"There's Foe's," Uncle Paul points, as we pass a building on the right, heading toward sugar heaven.

"*Foe's?*" I say, missing the sign and not recognizing the word.

"Fraternal Order of Eagles," he says, pointing to the F.O.E. #555 sign that we just passed. I see it now in my rearview mirror. "Easier to just say *Foe's*," he adds.

We see Steinly's and Pillitiere's, some of our other Firestone Park haunts. Uncle Paul thinks Pillitiere's has the best hash browns in the city. We went to lunch there once, and the staff swarmed around him when he came in the building. *It's Mr. Burnham!* the servers said, and some of the regulars sitting in booths greeted Mr. Burnham, too.

No one seemed to know his real name. After things settled down, I asked Uncle Paul what was going on.

He told me he always ordered hash browns here, and people got tired of hearing him say to burn 'em. It saved time just to tell the kitchen crew that Mr. Burnham had arrived.

We stop when we come to Krispy Kreme, and my uncle nearly tumbles from the car, hurrying so fast.

"Pick out a dozen for yourself," I tell him.

Uncle Paul comes here with his cousin Ruthie sometimes (he calls her "Cuz"), and people know him.

"Custard," he says. "But give me fresh ones."

Our young clerk heads toward the oven in the kitchen and counts out twelve custard doughnuts, hot to the touch.

He orders a cup of coffee. "Make it fresh!" he reminds the girl. "I don't like second-hand."

We climb in the car and head toward Grant Street and then downtown.

This is where the grain mills were when I was young. Mills had been in Akron in some form since Ferdinand Schumacher started making homemade oatmeal with a hand-operated mill rigged up in his grocery store, sometime in the mid-1800s. Not many years later, his mills were all over town and Schumacher was the "Oatmeal King of America." He'd made Akron famous.

My great-grandfather, my great-uncles, and my grandfather all worked in the Schumacher mills at one time. In fact, some of them came to this country just to work the mills. Schumacher put Akron on the manufacturing map before rubber did, and employed generations of German immigrants, like the men in my family, to make a product people missed from home.

Uncle Paul knows all about the mills. I point to the hotel at Quaker Square, located on the site where the Quaker Oats factory was originally housed, and ask him what else he remembers about oats. He tells

me a story I've never heard before. My great-grandfather Haberkost
hired out his horse to turn a millstone. He'd walk that horse down
Grant Street every day toward Exchange and the mills, then walk it
home with him at night. Or maybe it was his hired hand who did the
walking. My uncle can't remember. One day, though, shortly after the
streetcar line was extended to Grant, the horse collided with its iron
rival. The noise of the car had startled the horse, and the animal had
veered into it. The car ripped the left flank from the horse's body and
it had to be shot. It was struck near the corner of Grant and Cross, my
uncle tells me.

I wonder if its hooves touched any part of Cross when it collided
with the car. I try to imagine the horse falling, and watch it struggle to
keep its hooves on the ground. I see the blood racing from its flank
and then I see the horse folding in upon itself, joint by joint, until it's
not a horse at all. It tries to rise, but can't, and exhales a final shriek
that's higher and louder than the noon whistle of the Burkhardt Brewery. Its legs give a little flutter in the air, and then stop.

I don't understand great beasts, or how they bear what they do.
And I don't understand this corner, or what happened to Eddie any
better. I think of the irony that the spot where my great-grandfather's
horse was hit was nearly the identical place where Eddie was struck.
A horse torn open by a streetcar and a boy crushed beneath an auto-
mobile.

They're different kinds of tragedy, but the horse now seems to me
some horrible harbinger of my family's fate.

Tragic corners appear in everyone's life. Every family has one.
Cross and Grant certainly was ours. Cross, paved in its original brick,
always reminds me that it's one of the city's oldest roads. When I look
at it, I see Akron's history, and I see my own. Most of all, though, I see
Eddie. I imagine the toe of his shoe caught in the brick when he fell to

the ground and was pulled under a car. I imagine him tangled up with the body of a horse, his head nuzzled under the great beast's neck, his small hand reaching for its mane, wanting more than anything to pull himself onto the creature's back so they both can ride away.

There was another catastrophe on Cross and Grant that I've known about for a long while, but I've never connected it with my family's history before now. It seems an eerie part of the sequence.

People who study Akron, even casual historians like me, know that in 1890 a tornado blew down Cross on its way out of town. It's known as the famous Akron tornado, and it did terrible damage on the corner of Cross and Grant. It announced itself in banks of clouds and a sudden fall in temperature. It formed somewhere in the Main Street area but quickly twisted east to Washington and Thornton. The sky turned into angry purples, greens, grays, and finally a steamy white as the funnel shifted to a higher gear, roared straight down Cross Street, and damaged or destroyed every home and every piece of property that stood in its way.

The cone grew black as it sucked earth and debris into the air. Houses lost roofs and window glass. Walls blew off and some homes were turned half around or twisted from their foundations like screws. The storm peeled bark from trees.

The tornado tore north on Grant. It seemed lost, or perhaps it had just stepped aside to gather strength. One home, flipped completely upside down, looked like Noah's Ark ready to float away. There are drawings of it in Akron history books. The tornado mangled Turner Hall, Akron's German center. The roof flew away in the wind, the glass in its windows turned to powder, the siding sharpened into slivers and shot like silvery sticks high into the air. It struck the Burkhardt Brewery, disassembling its barns, icehouses, and sheds, and then yanked giant trees from the ground, snapping their roots like celery sticks.

A horse hitched to a wagon near the corner of Cross and Grant died instantly when the storm broke an electric wire and it fell across the animal's neck. Died just about where the Haberkost horse would die a few years later, and Eddie, sixty years after that.

Uncle Paul isn't thinking about the tornado, though, and pulls me back to Quaker Square.

"Quaker Oats!" Uncle Paul says, looking up at the hotel in front of us. He salutes. "How 'bout that!"

The Quaker man with the black hat and apple cheeks came to Akron after the Jumbo Mill burned down. His thirty-six silos, now hotel rooms and specialty shops, rose on charred ground. An empire of mills. There are no oats here now, except perhaps in a restaurant inside the complex, but my uncle is looking at silos and smelling the grain. I can tell.

"Do you remember the odor, Uncle Paul? I do."

I see him look over at me, lifting that great scruffy eyebrow of his.

"Sure," he says. "But there was the smell of hops, too, on Grant Street. It was strong. You must remember the hops, Babe. You lived as close to the brewery as the Steurers did."

I don't know what hops are, but I know they have something to do with beer. Uncle Paul has complicated things.

"What do hops smell like?" I say, trying to remember.

"They smell like Grandpa Haberkost," he says.

CHAPTER 13

I look "hops" up on the Internet. The entry says they are the flower cones of a plant, and they flavor and stabilize beer. Hops are bitter, to balance the sweetness of malt. They smell like orange peel, or herbs, basil and thyme. I imagine their raw flavor.

I've never especially liked beer, but I think of the bars I've been in, and smell the hops. There was always a sour aftertaste, and now I have a name for it. I realize that I'm afraid of men who carry the fragrance of hops in the weave of their clothes. I can't remember ever feeling otherwise. To me, it's the smell of danger and humiliation. It was the smell of a distant uncle in New York who cupped my breast in the foyer of his house late one night, of a balding relative in Connecticut who came into the guest room where I was staying (only a little girl) to French kiss me before I fell asleep, of my father when he returned to my mother and me after poker games on Friday nights with his pockets turned inside out and his big lips trembling, and of men who have lied to me. My uncle Paul drank only Pepsi or Coke—both of which he referred to as "Popsicles." On social occasions, he bought Hop 'N Gator for guests who drank. I'm pretty sure he didn't know it had twenty-five percent more alcohol than other beers. He just knew it wasn't officially a beer product, and he liked that.

My uncle is right about Grandpa. Hops *was* his cologne. I remember now. I hadn't thought of this before because Grandpa Haberkost

Carol and author in the living room of Grandmother's house

never smelled like anything else. To say he smelled like hops would be to say he smelled like Grandpa. Grandpa would sit in the parlor with a dark bottle of beer in one hand and a smoke in the other, and rock. His chair was positioned exactly in the center of the room and surrounded by a Lionel train. A beer and a cigarette were extensions of each hand.

There aren't any pictures of us gathered in Grandpa's parlor, because children never entered it. We played in the living room at the front of the house. I have a few pictures taken in the dining room of Grandma's house (no one ever called it "Grandpa's house") that show sober faces on each side of a narrow rectangular table, looking up at the camera, waiting for the click so that suspended spoons can finish the trip to half-opened mouths. But most of the photos were taken in the living room. It had wallpaper with huge feathery leaves (I remember pink, but it could have been blue or tan), a dark sofa (with a silver mirror over it), and windows that faced the east (Merkl's Gas Station) and the south (Crislips' Grocery Store). There was a floor lamp, one table lamp, and a figurine of a Dutch girl. The only painting in Grandma's house was the cheap lithograph from Cincinnati of Millet's *The Angelus* that my mother inherited, and then I inherited from her.

Grandpa is in none of the pictures of the living room. He sat in *his* parlor. The only time he moved was to sit on *his* porch.

I don't think it was ever people who drew him outside. He wasn't the friendly type. When he wore a hat, I never saw him tip it.

And it probably wasn't the odor of oats that caused him to leave his rocking chair.

It was that other smell that came wafting up the street from the Burkhardt Brewery.

CHAPTER 14

In my blood is the blood of my grandfather. Yet, I know almost nothing about him, except for beer, cigarettes, and white shirts.

In one of my mother's family folders, I found August's remembrance card from his funeral. He was buried by the Eckard-Baldwin Funeral Home, where the Haberkosts often go. I'm *sure* I attended. I must have. I went to Anna Haberkost's funeral in 1959. To my grandpa Coyne's funeral in 1966. To my grandma Coyne's funeral in 1972. I remember them all. I would surely have gone to August's in 1961. I was in ninth grade at the time, and should remember the day we buried him. I don't.

There was a mystery about August that no one ever explained to the children. It might account for my inability to retrieve any memory of his burial day. Shortly before Eddie died, we kids noticed that Grandpa wasn't in the house anymore. This was the early 1950s. I'm not sure who noticed it first, or if we even talked about it, but we began to move more freely through the rooms. We could enter the house by the front door and pass by the parlor into the kitchen now. We didn't have to use the back door to get there, didn't need to circumvent Grandpa's room. We began to play in the parlor once Grandpa left, and reclaimed the train that circled his rocking chair. It was Eddie's train, but Eddie seldom got to watch it run. It may have crossed

August Haberkost in a white shirt, rolled at the sleeves, with Anna

our minds that Grandpa was dead, but no one ever said so. His absence certainly never worried us.

Nine years later, Grandpa came back to town in a hearse.

Even as a young adult, I wasn't curious about where Grandpa had gone. That had to wait until I started my trips back to Goosetown with Uncle Paul. When I became curious about Goosetown, I had to become curious about August Haberkost. Grandpa had more of Goosetown in him than any of us. He was born in Goosetown in 1880, just six years after his grandmother arrived from Mecklenburg, Germany.

By the time I realized there was a mystery, almost no one was left to help me solve it.

My mother never mentioned her father's vanishing act when she was alive, and since she's dead, I can't ask. Her six brothers and sisters are dead, too. The only other people left are the two spouses of August's daughters—Uncle Paul (who had married Ruth) and Scotty (Marie's second or third husband, depending on how you count).

I must have felt that Grandpa's funeral was the funeral of a stranger. I don't remember funerals of strangers. Probably the only surprise of the day was finding out that Grandpa hadn't been dead for the past nine years.

"Where did he go?" I now ask Uncle Paul.

"I don't know, Babe. Wish I could help you out. You'll probably need this for your book."

I notice my upper lip lifting a little too high, like the waitress at Steinly's Restaurant.

"Did *anyone* know? Surely someone—"

"Your mother collected money from her sisters every month. Just a few dollars is all Ruth and I ever paid. I think it was for Dad, but Ruth never said. Or I've forgotten."

"Did *anyone* ever visit him?"

"No. Not that I knew. *We* never did."

"Not in nine years?"

"No."

"That's a long time not to visit your *father*," I say. I don't mean to be unkind, but I can see my words have upset Uncle Paul a little.

"They didn't love him the way they did their mother. Ruth didn't, I know. That happens sometimes in families, and it's real sad. He was in a bad way."

"What do you mean?" I say.

"Oh, he was a *rascal!*" Uncle Paul says. He won't say that August was mean or that he drank too much. He told me once that sometimes sons-in-law stayed overnight in the Grant Street house to help Grandma, but when he said this, he couched it in a little laugh.

My uncle's word, "rascal," is meant to explain everything, but it just raises more questions in my mind. Why had this rascal left home? Where had he gone? Why didn't anyone tell us stories about Grandpa and the old days, like other grandchildren routinely got to hear? Why would his seven children refuse to utter his name after he left town? What did my uncle mean when he said that August was *in a bad way?*

"Isn't there anything more?" I ask.

"He pulled his own teeth with his fingers," Uncle Paul says. I see August sitting in his chair, jamming those tinsmith's fingers into his mouth. Without making a sound, he extracts a tooth. My uncle says the line without emotion, so I don't know how he feels about what my grandpa did. I can't tell if he admired August for the strength that let him pry the teeth right out of his jaw, or feared the brutality of the man.

"His hands were strong, but all tore up," he says. "He was a roofer. Did sheet metal work and was all cut up."

When I try to imagine my grandpa pulling his teeth, I see his fingers turn into snips, or thresher hooks, see them burrow down into the gum, watch them dig out a human tooth.

And now I see it there, a bloody thing with long, rotten roots. He's holding it between his index finger and his thumb, smiling, hoping someone will pass by the parlor so he can show them what he's done.

CHAPTER 15

Uncle Paul has had a big influence on my temperament. I try to make the best of things, just the way that he does. Mysteries don't all have to be dark. That's what I tell myself.

I want August to be a good man. I want the reason for his disappearance to surprise me in a pleasant way. I want to like him.

I make up a story in my head about Grandpa working on roofs all over town when he was young. I picture him as the Happy Artisan, singing his way off to work early on a sunny morning, with those strong hands of his swinging at his sides, architects' drawings tucked under an arm, his long legs and long gait moving him forward, his agile mind measuring every surface he sees in front of him. I like to think of him as tall and standing straight, not stooped over the way I see him in photographs. In my imagination, he has suspenders and little leather pants that come just above his knees. He wears a simple embroidered shirt. He looks like a herder in the Alps. He's a character in *Heidi*. He's my Alpen-grandfather, all goat's milk and mountain air.

This is the man who won Anna's heart.

Maybe she noticed his tools one day when he walked by her house on the way home from work. Maybe they were slung across his back, around his belt, and she saw them and thought the two of them could surely build a life with those. This man had a craft. A job. An income. A future. People always needed roofs. As Anna and August walked the streets together, maybe he pointed out the roofs he had laid, his cheeks bright with pride.

See that, Anna? I did that, he might have said.

I'd like a roof like that, August.

No leaks, Anna. Not when I build.

It's fine work. And maybe Anna took his hand, and that small gesture sealed everything.

Even a rascal doesn't have to be all bad. Hal Roach's *Little Rascals*—we Coynes watched them faithfully on our first TV—featured kids who were all cute in their way and made us laugh. Stymie and Spanky and Buckwheat and Alfalfa and Porky and Chubby. They were all mischievous, but not mean the way that Butch Bond, the local bully, was when he tormented them. Even Petey, the pit bull in the films, was adorable, with that circle around one eye.

CHAPTER 16

I'm afraid of what I'll find if I look too hard. The *Little Rascals*, after all, didn't turn out that well in real life. Carl "Alfalfa" Switzer was shot to death during an argument at the age of thirty-one. Chubby kept gaining weight and died when he was eighteen and three hundred pounds. William "Buckwheat" Thomas died of a heart attack before he was fifty. Even adorable Petey was poisoned, probably by someone with a grudge against Harry Lucenay, his owner and trainer.

My uncle's rosy view is born from humility. He knows the world's natural acts are sometimes horrible, and that they can crush people. He tries not to be too hard on them, and says it's not for him to judge.

My *own* optimism, I'm afraid, is born of arrogance. I don't want to find something dark in Grandpa's past that embarrasses me. Lately I've read many memoirs full of stories about family atrocities. One writer found out her grandfather had been in the KKK and participated in a lynching. Another writer learned that a close relative of his had held an office in the Nazi party. Their stories made me cringe.

Embarrassment can seep inside, and turn to shame. I don't want that to happen. I don't know how I could feel the same about myself if I found out that a grandfather, someone whose genes I carried, had hanged black people on a courthouse square, or had driven Jews into cattle cars.

How could I be untainted by something like that, even though we were separated by a generation or two? When does blood thin out enough so that new generations no longer see the stain on their cheeks—feel the burn—when they think about atrocious acts of their ancestors?

I'd rather perceive Grandpa as the Happy Artisan. I want him to be the progenitor of my own craft. I want him to have been the best roofer in Akron, and to have made beautiful tin boxes with his able hands. I want to find one in an antique store one day, with his initials scratched into the back. *A. E. J. H.* Maybe in the shape of a small cricket box I can put above the fireplace, to bring me luck. People will ask me about it, and I'll tell the stories.

But there isn't any box.

I already know that Grandpa wasn't a character from a Disney film. There *were* leaks in his house. There were always leaks. I remember several in the living room. In even soft winds, shingles flew off the roof of the roofer's house. The porch sagged and needed paint. The cellar doors buckled and were nearly unusable. The front steps were caving in. There were holes in the screens as big as a calf's eye. I can't remember the sound of my grandparents' voices, but I do remember the sounds of a house in decay: the creak of the boards, popping of doors you had to pull too hard, the drip of water from broken faucets, the rip of fabric as a screen caught the edge of my skirt or my blouse, moth wings beating inside the shades of Grandma's table lamp at night.

I was seldom comfortable in Grandma's house.

It's the same discomfort I feel now, as I begin to track Grandpa down. You can't have lived in a place as long as August Haberkost lived in Goosetown without having left a few tracks. He disappeared in the early 1950s, but he couldn't pack seventy years in a suitcase before he left town, could he? Even Houdini couldn't do that.

CHAPTER 17

"What do you remember about August?" I ask my cousin Carol.

"I'd go out of my way to get out of his way," she says. She lived in Grandma's house after her mother's divorce (there wasn't money to rent a place of their own), so she knew Grandpa much better than I did.

In a letter, I ask an elderly nephew of Grandpa's who's still living a little south of Summit County the same thing. "Uncle Augie didn't enter much into family affairs and we surely did our best not to upset him," he writes back. Augie's nephew is a very formal and proper man, and our family's genealogist. I don't know what I'd do without the help he's given me with family history all these years, but he's prone to restraint when you ask him something that's too personal. The way he puts it, August had a "condition," and, he says, this condition "was 'self-inflicted,' and must have begun at an early age." I'm sure he's talking about alcohol, but the word never appears in his letter.

The word *alcohol* never appeared in family conversations, either.

I next ask Scotty what he remembers. Scotty has a good memory and spent a lot of time in the Grant Street house during his long engagement to my aunt Marie. He tells me he should be able to recall a few things about his father-in-law, if I just give him time. Nothing comes to him right away.

Scotty is like Uncle Paul—he never says much that's critical. He was so in love with Marie all his life, so glad to finally marry her, that

Aunt Marie and Scotty on their wedding day

he seldom judged her family. He was just happy to have one, so he never looked too hard at the Haberkosts.

"Did August ever do anything nice for anyone?" I ask.

He tilts his head, and tells me about the day that Grandpa fixed Eddie's train. That seems to be proof for him that the man had a heart.

August walked into the Grant Street house, Scotty says, and accidentally stepped on the Lionel train tracks in the parlor with his boot, and broke a switch. He spent an entire afternoon repairing the part.

Making it good as new. "He fixed it for Eddie," Scotty tells me. It's a sweet story, and I'm glad Scotty has remembered it.

But just *one* happy story? My grandpa lived to the age of eighty-one and, as far as I can tell, *one* person has *one* unqualified good memory of the man.

Something in me begins to wonder if even this one story is true. Is Scotty telling me everything about that day? Has he forgotten some of it? Was he there to witness it? Or did August tell him his own version of the story on the porch of the Grant Street house much later—weeks after the accident occurred? I've seen before how stories about fixing things get revised.

Someone might say, "I put up the Christmas tree this year," "I fixed the lamp," "I repaired the garage door," or "I installed the basketball net," but they leave out the anger and the obscenities and the threats and the mean accusations hurled at other people who might have gotten (or been) in their way. My father once took it upon himself to "repair" a window molding that had come loose in our Evergreen Avenue house. By the third hour into the repair, my mother was weeping by my father's side (still unable to get him to stop), I was running from room to room emptying ashtrays into our glossy green cigarette butler (trying to stay out of the way), and my father was prying off the entire window frame, stripped to his boxer shorts and undershirt and screaming at everyone (including people who weren't in the living room). My mother forgave Tom Coyne almost everything because he was *just a big stubborn Irishman*. But she didn't speak to him for three days after he destroyed our living room. Before the incident was over, a company came out to install a new window and my mother and I visited a decorating store to pick out new wallpaper for the living room, because Tom Coyne had destroyed the old paper during his assault on the window frame. The story is funny to tell now, but I'm not sure a house or a family ever recovers from episodes like this.

At least August's story ended well. He was a finer craftsman than my dad, there's little doubt of that. *Most* people were. But perhaps neither story really had a happy ending. You can sometimes repair things without fixing them.

So *maybe*. Maybe August walked into his house and the parlor drapes were drawn. It was dark, and he stepped on Eddie's train. He felt such remorse about breaking the switch that he tried to repair it before Eddie found out. He knew how much his grandson loved the train. Eddie had few other toys. Grandpa gathered his tools, returned to his rocking chair, set his beer down, and tinkered and soldered until everything worked as well as it had before his boot crushed the switch.

But Scotty is a nostalgic man, and maybe that's not what happened at all. Scotty is a sucker for a sweet story.

Here's a second version.

Maybe half drunk, in the middle of the day, August stumbled into his house, and then into the room with the train. He heard the mantle clock strike three and realized he'd forgotten something. It wasn't morning anymore, and it should have been. He looked at his hands and saw the calluses, and then at his feet and saw his heavy work boots, and suddenly remembered he'd been hired to fix a roof downtown at ten o'clock, but he was hours late, and the company would let him go. If not today, then tomorrow, or by the end of the month. It had happened before. His wife would point her grim face at him when she found him in the room, and her anger would spill into his meat that night and make it tough. Thinking about all this prevented him from thinking about anything else, and so he didn't and stepped on the track and heard the switch snap in two.

He knew the sound. He was a tinner, so he knew what he had done before he sat in the chair and reached for the damaged part. Maybe Eddie was home, saw the switch in pieces in his grandpa's cupped hand, and knew the train had reached the end of the Grant Street line. The child cried, and then the child howled, and Grandpa screamed and the child cried harder still and ran behind a chair in the living room and couldn't stop, couldn't bear one more broken thing. And Grandpa reached behind the chair and grabbed the child with his other hand and Grandma came running and screamed for him to stop and he knew he had to end these awful sounds, so he pushed his wife onto the sofa, smacked the child's head, hard, and went to get his tools. He found the soldering gun he'd planned to take to work before he'd gone to get a beer and then lost track of time. He found his mallet and the scissors that cut through metal. He melded and fused and shaped the switch until it was as good as new. The metal train on the metal track soon made both the crying and his wife's hard breathing stop.

Both versions have the same ending. The train gets fixed. But sometimes a story has little to do with the way it ends. The train might run again, but down the road everything could derail.

CHAPTER 18

Ink.

That's what the truth distills into, and the place where truth finally must be found. I have to search for ink to find my grandpa.

I learned this from my uncle Paul, and his walnut tree. The tree grew in his backyard on Ivy Place, but it's gone now. My uncle loved that black walnut.

We hated the tree, though. It didn't belong in a kid's world. It stained the blacktop where we played basketball, formed green slime on the grass after the walnuts fell (we couldn't even run without worrying about that goo), crusted our knees with a substance as brown and dense as scabs, and wasn't good to eat (none of us had the time or strength to crack through all those layers to get to the edible nuts the squirrels loved).

When we told Uncle Paul it was just a nasty tree, he would go to the garage and bring out vials of black ink. The garage was his laboratory. He collected the husks of the walnuts there, let them rot to mush, and strained the viscid substance into midnight dye through a piece of cheesecloth.

The Pilgrims made their ink this way, he told us. And then he took a feather and carved a point on the tip with a pocket knife. The neighbor's pet crow sometimes flew to him on his porch and left behind tokens that became my uncle's quills.

He dipped it in.

I don't remember what he wrote, but I remember the ink. It was so thick that it looked more like blood than ink. So rich it bled through paper. So dark that it bore no resemblance to the substance in the Scripto bottles that sat in the inkwells of our desks in elementary school.

I thought my uncle was a magician that day.

He knew how to turn things into ink, even the walnuts from his own backyard.

CHAPTER 19

The history of the Haberkosts flows in the ink of the *Akron Beacon Journal*. My family has read that paper since my great-great-grandparents, Jochim and Sophia Haberkost, arrived from Germany. My son was a *Beacon* reporter for ten years, and I've been a subscriber all my life. An index to old issues of the paper, from 1841 to 1939, was prepared by Works Progress Administration (WPA) workers. All I have to do is crank the reel to "Haberkost, August," and I can see what my grandpa was up to. I've used the index before to find out about Akron history, but I never thought to search for my own family. Now, I can't stop cranking microfilm and find myself heading to Bierce Library at the University of Akron almost every day.

Nineteenth-century journalism contained more gossip than a New York tabloid does now. There were so many Haberkosts running around town that one of them was always in the news. There are columns of entries for Haberkosts in the index.

I find a story about something August did shortly after he married Grandma in 1904. It catches my eye. I load the reel of microfilm and begin to turn.

Just ten days after his wedding, August stole my grandma's watch. The headline is sensational: "Pawned the Watch and Caused Trouble, Haberkost Disturbed His Domestic Relations by His Actions."

Wedding picture of August and Anna, October 12, 1904

Was this what Uncle Paul meant by "rascal"?

He told his wife he took the watch to be repaired. But time passed, and August came back, but the watch did not.

The headline probably doesn't contain as much sensation as there was in Anna's home the day she found out she was married to a rapscallion. A common thief. *Rascal* squared.

It was November when Anna discovered August had pawned her watch. Risked everything to buy a little alcohol, the story says. The truth came out, and August was summoned to police court. He promised to fix matters with the pawnbroker, to fix matters with Anna, and to get the watch back and pay the costs. The court was satisfied. "When this is done this case will be dismissed," the paper says. And the story ends.

But does it? Could Anna and August just continue being newly-weds, and pretend nothing had changed?

Was it just her watch he had pawned, or the precious time she had so eagerly promised to give him? A lifetime of hours, of days, of years?

I think I own Grandma's watch, the one August sold. When my mother died, I found several watches in a drawer. There was the old square Hamilton Annabelle wore. But there was a Bulova I'd never seen. It's sized for a wrist smaller than my mother's, but even *I* couldn't fit it over my hand. The Bulova is made for tiny bones. It has a silver clasp and narrow strips of black elastic for a band. Its face is long, framed in hammered silver, like a portrait is. It's an old face, like my grandma's. Long and narrow and flat. Expressionless, except for the metal hands that remind you time will coldly spin away.

The watch makes me sad when I look at it. It's a funny story in the *Beacon*, but I wonder if Anna was ever amused. August stole my grandma's heart, and then ten days later he stole her watch. He didn't seem to notice there was any difference between the two. He was on a roll.

First a heart.

Next a watch.

What would he steal next?

CHAPTER 20

I'm pretty sure Uncle Paul won't go with me to try to find out more about Grandpa, so I'm not surprised when he tells me he's a little tired the morning that I call to ask. He's eating his cornflakes. It's not the "crunch, crunch, crunch" of the flakes that gives this away (he always pours coffee on them and lets them soak a few minutes before he eats them, so the cereal doesn't make any noise). It's the sound of his spoon hitting the bowl, like a little rhythm band.

It's not that he's afraid to go with me. *I'm* the one who's fearful. He's just worn out from probing things, and doesn't want to do that anymore. Ever since the deaths of Ruth and Edith, and my mother and father too, he's retreated some. Become less adventurous, less eager to dig too deeply into things. When they probed the people he loved most in the whole world, probed the darkest corners of their bodies, they found cancer cells or, in the case of my mother and Edith, tangles and plaques that would destroy their brains. He knows how to face those things—no one is more valiant than my uncle Paul or has spent more time at hospitals with the sick, or *being* sick—but he doesn't want new worries. *I'm tuckered out* is what he always says, and he says it when I call.

My uncle is certainly not afraid of dying. Dying doesn't worry him, and never has. He had numerous surgeries even as a young man for a cyst on his neck (by the time doctors figured out how to stop it from seeping, the War was over and he couldn't enlist), several operations for varicose veins, the aneurysm that almost killed him (he was changing a flat tire on the side of a road when it happened), and three heart bypasses. When I was very young, I used to think he had his own room at the hospital, in addition to a house in Firestone Park. I often went to see him. He was completely calm through everything—every test, every emergency, every operation—as if danger were no different from grace. He was more relaxed than the priests who visited him, more patient with those old veins and bones of his than his doctors were, in better spirits than any of his friends who called (and there were long lines of them). He's had Extreme Unction so often that his forehead has begun to shine.

He knows a lot more about dying than I do. That might be what's helped him survive so long.

Maybe one day I'll feel the way he does now. I won't be as eager to solve the riddles that perplex me. I won't need to ask so many questions or crank so many reels of microfilm or refuse to let the dead alone. I'll wait for news to come to me and spend my time dreaming only of past lovers and onion soup.

It isn't that he discourages me. He *wants* me to go. He just has no interest in riding along. He's finished his research, and he'll wait for me to tell him what's new. *What's new, Babe?!* he always says when he sees me, or when we talk on the phone. He'll never stop saying that. But unlike his coffee, he likes news second-hand now. He doesn't even read the sad stories on the front page of the newspaper anymore. It's just too hard.

"The lions in front might eat you!" he jokes, when I tell him I'm off to the Summit County Courthouse.

"No they won't," I say. "They're stone."

"Be careful, Babe!"

CHAPTER 21

I drive downtown and park in the lot across from the courthouse. It's a little lonely without my uncle Paul. If he were with me now, we'd have the roof wide open. He loves my car, especially the sunroof. He makes me open the roof on nice days before we start out. *I didn't know you had a convertible,* he always says when I press the switch that causes the glass panel on my Corolla to retract.

I have some change in my pocket in case there are documents I want to reproduce, and I finger the coins.

I see the stone lions that Uncle Paul has warned me to be careful of, caught forever in an angry growl at the edge of the street, guarding the courthouse on the hill. The lower steps that once reached all the way to the lions have been removed. But the statues remain. The courthouse behind them looks just as fierce as the lions do—just the way it always did when I was a girl and stared at it. There's nothing friendly about it, and for a minute it reminds me of an enormous mausoleum, with only death inside. I want to run away. Built from sandstone harvested from local quarries, it looks like a gigantic cut in the side of a mountain, something from underground with all the strata displayed.

Winding my way past marble pillars to the inside stairs, I feel the guilt and shame buried in this place. I remember a story about Nathaniel Hawthorne. Because his great-great grandfather John Hathorne was a merciless judge in the Salem Witch Trials, Hawthorne changed the spelling of his own name by adding a *w*. At least, that's the story I've heard. He wiped away the crime with that simple stroke. Hawthorne believed, as we well know, in the power of a letter, whether it was a scarlet *A* or the *w* of his own name. The Haberkosts changed the *c* in their name to a *k* shortly after they arrived from Germany, to Americanize it, I suppose. Maybe the change was made *for* them, on Ellis Island. But by the time their naturalization papers were finalized, the *k* was permanent. I'm not sure there's much left for me to alter in the spelling of the name anymore, should I need to. I'll have to figure out some other way to hide.

Grandpa was a heavy drinker. Maybe even a drunk. But drinking as much as Grandpa did was common among Akron men at the turn of the century, especially when you lived across the street from a brewery, or a bar. Looking through old city directories a few days before, I learned the drugstore on Cross and Grant had formerly been a saloon. When Grandpa was a young man, there was both a brewery *and* a bar across the street from his house.

I think about all the stories I've read in the *Beacon* about alcohol in Akron, and about drunks in my own family. There are articles about the formation of the Anti-Saloon League, and about Akron ministers from First Church of Christ and Grace Reformed campaigning for temperance and urging saloons to close on Sunday afternoons. There are also many stories about August's uncles and cousins. Even the uncle for whom my grandpa was named—August J., patrolman #12 on the Akron police force—couldn't avoid the temptation of the downtown bars he patrolled. In 1904, the year of Grandpa's wedding and his first prank, Officer Haberkost was suspended for seven days. While on duty one Friday night he had entered Germann & Sutter's saloon on North College Street and drunk whiskey with two other officers amidst a crowd of travelers waiting for trains.

The saloon was opposite Union Depot and had a restaurant attached that served meals at all hours—the Union Café.

On my way to the courthouse, I visited Grandpa's grave. It's not far from downtown, but this was another trip Uncle Paul didn't want to make, so I thought I'd work it in. My uncle told me how to find the cemetery and gave me general directions to the gravesite. I thought I'd found it, but I wasn't sure. The stone was *completely* overgrown, almost entirely hidden from view. There was nothing visible but a single sharp edge, so it took a groundskeeper to confirm I was standing on Grandpa's plot.

My uncle had insisted I take scissors along, and now I knew why. I trimmed and pried, slowly clearing the glassy surface. I hadn't known that August and Anna shared a single stone. But there they were together. A common marker, *Haberkost* carved at the top. *August E., 1880–1961* in a small rectangle on the left, *Anna M., 1880–1959* in a rectangle of the same size on the right. No epitaph had been chosen.

Not far from the Haberkost plot I spotted the grave of one of the most famous people in Akron's Mt. Peace Cemetery, Dr. Bob, co-founder of Alcoholics Anonymous. I couldn't miss his large monument-style stone. Dr. Robert Holbrook Smith appeared to be the only dead person in the whole cemetery permitted a planter of live flowers in a vase beside his grave. *Honesty. Purity. Unselfishness. Love.* Those were the words on the vase. People from all over knew about Dr. Bob's grave, and it was perfectly kept. I'd read for years in the *Beacon* about the annual parade and celebration that commemorated Dr. Bob, including a walk through Mt. Peace Cemetery by all the pilgrims who would come to honor him. I wondered how August's life might have been different if he'd met Dr. Bob above the ground, rather than below.

I'm still thinking of August Haberkost and Dr. Bob as I enter an upstairs room of the courthouse. I decide first to check the Intoxication Dockets. Grandpa's name isn't anywhere. No one ever found him rolling in a ditch, besotted and confused. He didn't make a public spectacle of himself, at least. I'm safe.

I leaf through the criminal dockets next, but I'm almost sure now that Grandpa's name won't be there. The Intoxication Dockets suggest he was behaving himself. But I want to make sure. I want to be thorough. I'm still worried about his problem with theft, but I begin to think it ended with the warning the court gave him after he pawned the watch.

Before today, I didn't know criminal records were public documents. I didn't know much of anything about the courthouse. I spotted the records by chance, moving up and down rows, wandering between rooms. I'd been inside the building only once before when my husband and I applied for a marriage license. My only other brush with the courthouse had occurred a few years back, and it surprises me that I suddenly remember it. Sitting in a line of traffic on Broadway Street, I'd seen a row of young boys, few of them older than twenty, dressed in orange jumpsuits, chained together at the ankles and wrists, moving slowly from the back of the courthouse toward a bus that was probably transporting them to the county jail after sentencing. They were about my son's age, and I felt responsible for them, tender, even. I didn't want to see among them any boys who might bear some resemblance to my child—his posture, his hair, his resonant voice. I didn't want the lions to come to life and consume a child of mine.

I feel danger again as I hold something in my hand I had hoped to never find. Grandpa has surprised me.

He *was* a felon after all.

This time, he had gone to jail. His criminal record hides in a tall book, dated November 14, 1926. Twenty-two years after his first recorded theft, he stole again.

When he committed his second crime, my grandfather was not a young man like the boys I saw dressed in orange. He could have been those boys in 1904, when he stole my grandma's watch, but not now. He was forty-six, and he'd broken into the Freight House of the Pennsylvania Railroad Company with the full intention of stealing railroad property. He'd been caught and arrested and, when he couldn't pay a $1500 bond, sentenced to the city jail for a month.

That jail isn't there anymore, but before it was torn down I'd visited it during a field trip in elementary school. We were excited when we learned that we would go. We all loved playing cowboys and Indians, cops and robbers, and we thought this would be the kind of jail we saw on TV shows, a cute little town jail on a dirt street with wooden walkways for women who wore wide skirts and carried parasols. There was always a jail in Westerns, with a sheriff at a desk, a cell with a bed, and one window facing the street. There was a white curtain on it that the sheriff or the jailor sometimes pulled back to see who was riding into town to cause trouble, or to look at a pretty girl walking by. The jail in the shows was a little like a dollhouse, or someone's front room. There were a few wanted posters on the wall, along with a couple of rifles in a rack, but always a pot-bellied stove in a corner to keep people warm.

We hadn't studied jails or the prison system in our elementary school. The subject wasn't in any of our textbooks. All we talked about in class were dairy cows and how milk was made, the way trucks worked (someone's dad drove a real tractor into the parking lot and we climbed up on it), and the lives of firemen (this, too, occasioned a field trip to the local firehouse on Brown Street). Jails never were mentioned. Neither, of course, was alcohol.

The old Akron jail wasn't like those in cowboy shows on the TV. The Akron jail looked like a European castle from the outside, solid stone, with arches on the doors and turrets at the corners. As you approached it, though, the heavy grates on the windows became visible. Inside, it smelled like pee.

Summit County Jail, 1902 (Courtesy Summit County Historical Society, Akron, Ohio)

When I visited in the late 1950s, I had no idea that my grandpa had once been kept inside the thick, damp walls. I was sure that the people we saw in those cells had nothing to do with the people who lived in the neighborhoods I came from. They couldn't have been little girls' fathers or grandpas. They were not like anyone in my family. Not like the Haberkosts and the Coynes. They were not like me.

But Grandpa was a resident of the Summit County Jail for thirty days.

Grandpa was a thief. A real, live, convicted criminal.

He needed money for beer, and there wasn't any. So he had to figure something out.

CHAPTER 22

When you find a thief in your family, you're forced to imagine the thief in yourself. You can't pretend you aren't related to a felon.

I've stolen things.

A dill pickle wrapped in wax paper from a friend's lunch box in elementary school.

A tube of red lipstick from my mother, which I buried beside a tree close to the Harvey Firestone monument, and dug up on my way to school.

Money I failed to pay when a cashier undercharged me, though I spotted her error right away and knew what I owed.

Some orange daylilies from someone else's woods, which I boldly planted in my front yard.

Forty dollars I found by the gazebo in town and didn't turn in. I had no spending money the week I found it and needed some. I called it *good luck*.

Too much of my mother's time.

Too much of my father's pride.

Too many favors from everyone, without sufficient gratitude.

CHAPTER 23

Other documents begin to unfold, like those old postcard book-
lets from Florida with sixteen colored photographs. Hold the top one
head-high, the others flip-flop down, all the way to the floor.

Part of me wants to stop this search, but I can't. There's more to
the story, and I know it. It's inside this building.

I go to the same year as the Pennsylvania Railroad break-in, this
time in the civil records. In a large, heavy book of entries I find a divorce summons. It's a petition by Anna Haberkost.

I can hardly believe that this document exists, that my shy, silent
grandma spoke up. Announced, *Enough!* While August was in jail
cooling off and drying out, Anna filed for divorce. She accused him of
not being able to hold a job because of alcohol and claimed he was an
unfit spouse. The Clerk of Courts wrote it all down. *He has refused
and still refuses to go to work and earn money for the support of plaintiff and her children with the result that she and they have been de-
prived of the necessities of life.*

I think of my mother telling me that at Christmas each child received a single orange.

Anna told something else to her attorneys, and to the court. She
told a secret I'm sure she had kept from everyone else, kept hidden in
her angry heart. *He has threatened to kill his oldest son, Howard.*

Howard was eighteen when Anna filed her petition. I don't know what kind of boy he was. Perhaps he was old enough to finally stand up to his father or old enough to begin to resemble him. Maybe when August looked at him he saw a foe. Maybe August saw himself a little more clearly than he had before. Either way, through fear or self-repulsion, he may have screamed his anger and hatred through the ·house, a house where Betty, age three, Leroy, age five, and Marie, only nine years old, also lived. August may have struck the boy. Beat him. Lost control and said he would kill him.

But Howard was still a boy, and August had forgotten that. He'd grown tall, and perhaps his size had confused August. A boy lived inside the body of a man, but perhaps August saw only his height, and not his terrible fragility.

The sheriff delivered the summons to August in the jail, along with a restraining order, and I wonder what my grandpa must have thought when he read it and found out that the thin woman he had married (the woman with stick-figure arms—my arms!—a woman who could hardly keep a watch on her wrist) had hired attorneys Herberich, Burroughs, & Bailey. Because of them, he no longer could walk through his own front door. His home was still there, but someone had changed the magic word that rolled the stone away.

Where did Anna find the resolve to file for divorce in this great building? To walk a mile and a half up the Grant Street hill to East Exchange, then to Broadway and South High Street? To wind her way through the marble pillars on the first floor of the courthouse, then walk up a staircase whose steps were as wide and cold as those she must have remembered on the north bank of the ledge near Old Maid's Kitchen? To deliver her testimony to the Clerk of Courts, a stranger sitting at an enormous oak desk who was taking notes about the greatest intimacies of her life?

As I try to picture this, I realize I don't know her at all.

But one thing I *do* know. Something very close to a truth about my family is typed and stored between heavy leather covers on a shelf of civil records in the Summit County Courthouse. And it was Anna who put it there.

Is this story *mine* now, just because I've found it? The forty dollars and the daylilies weren't mine, even though I took them. Would Anna have asked me to return the volume to its shelf, to keep her story hidden for eternity in this dark, cool room?

Perhaps I should be silent and not ask for a copy. Ham was the son cursed by God and Noah for pointing out his father's drunkenness. Shem and Japheth refused to look at Noah full of the wine from his vineyard and covered him up by walking toward him backward with a cloth across their shoulders before dropping it. Noah blessed them for this, and cursed Ham for seeing him as he really was and telling his brothers. It would be so much easier for me, maybe so much better for others I love, if I just turn my back and cover August up, and let Anna be.

Even our families offer us few rewards for truth. From Noah to now, hasn't that always been the case? Sometimes the *most* we can hope for is their curse.

Perhaps I should let go of things that have yellowed and grown silent on a shelf over so many years.

Better to be silent?

Better to be still?

But I don't think that's the lesson here. Anna chose to speak. She couldn't bear the burden of her secrets anymore. Her first-born son was in deadly danger, and she was, too. She had this one chance to get away. With August in jail she could finally act, and so she walked a mile and a half and sat in a chair with a high, straight back, her hands folded in front of her, twisting the simple buttons of her cotton dress. It would have been a black dress. Anna usually wore black.

Then she stood.

Anger and sorrow and hatred and shame forced the first word up
her throat and out into the highest room that my grandmother had
ever stood in.

She was creating a public document. A public spectacle. Ending
silence with a signature. At the bottom of the petition, just below the
names of her lawyers, is her name in script. *Anna Haberkost.* It's the
only place and the only time I've ever seen her signature. Her script is
beautiful, every letter clear, with no embellishment. You can tell each
stroke was deliberate, yet, there's lightness in the way the final letters
float above the line.

She had chosen not to be private anymore. She had used her
name. What she said was said to the court, said to the city and the
county and the state. What she said was said to me.

CHAPTER 24

But Anna did not divorce August. When I was born in 1947, they were still married.

And so I wonder: If Anna could find the kind of courage it must have taken to file for divorce and make a public confession in the Summit County Courthouse, why would she withdraw her plea?

What could have happened that changed her mind? Perhaps the answer's in chronology?

On November 14, 1926, August Haberkost broke into the Freight House of the Pennsylvania Railroad Company.

A warrant for his arrest was issued by an Akron police officer on November 15, 1926.

August appeared before a municipal judge on November 16, 1926, and entered a plea of not guilty. On that day, unable to pay bond, he was sent to jail to await the action of the Grand Jury.

On November 17, 1926, Anna Haberkost filed for divorce in the office of the Clerk of the Court of Common Pleas of Summit County, and the State of Ohio.

On November 17, 1926, three orders were issued simultaneously: one requiring the defendant to pay alimony *in such sum as the court deems sufficient*; a second *restraining the defendant from conversing or attempting to converse with the plaintiff, from annoying and molesting plaintiff or attempting to do so, or from disposing or encumber-*

ing his property; a third charging him with *gross neglect and extreme cruelty*. The sheriff delivered the orders to August in the Akron City Jail. He charged seventy-five cents for his services and sixteen cents for mileage, at eight cents a mile.

The Grand Jury indicted August Haberkost on December 13, 1926.

His case went to court on December 22. At that time, he expressed a desire to change his plea to guilty. The court then chose not to sentence him, but to place him on probation for one year. It named as his probation officer the pastor of Concordia Evangelical Lutheran Church, a cousin of August's through marriage. These were the conditions of August's release:

That the defendant pay the costs of this prosecution.

That he refrain from drinking intoxicants.

That he obey the laws and ordinances of the place where he resides.

On an undated journal entry, there is one last notation about Anna's divorce proceedings: *Plaintiff dismisses this action without prejudice. No record. Costs paid.*

No record? The hearing to dismiss was not recorded. I will never know why Anna changed her mind. To the court, the matter was not important enough to preserve with words. Not important enough to justify a stenographer's time.

The court seems to have done what was most expedient. A deal had been struck. August would plead guilty, the pastor of the Lutheran church in Goosetown would assume full responsibility for him (when I was growing up, I knew the pastor, a gentle man who tended a garden, played a trombone, and owned a dozen thoroughbred sheep), August would abide by the court's directive. The State would be rid of the expense of another prisoner, a cell would be available for someone else, and August Haberkost would be home by Christmas.

But I can only guess why Anna changed *her* plea, and wonder. Was it also expediency? Was it just easier to take August back? Easier than what?

CHAPTER 25

Each day, Uncle Paul positions himself close to a window in his Grant Street house. He sits in his sofa most of the time, next to the recliner where Ginger sleeps, right by the east window. From here he can see his backyard, a slender mountain ash tree growing in the center. It's not as big as the London Planetrees he sees from his west window, but the ash reminds him of Ivy Place, so that's why I think he likes the east window best. He started the ash from the seed of a mature tree on his first property in the Park, so in a way it's what remains of Ruth. I think he brought it here, to the house of his second wife, to remind him of Ruth.

When I ring the bell, he seldom hears it, so I just walk in.

"Constantinopleoctanishangdoodlesockpipergazelle," I yell, so I don't startle him. That's the password he taught us as kids. No common thief would shout anything quite like that, so he knows it's me.

Today he's sitting in his sofa working the morning crossword puzzle in the *Beacon*. William Safire's *Freedom* is opened on the table, weighted down by a heavy magnifying glass. A week ago he was reading a thick Civil War history. He also likes Louis L'Amour, Jack London, and Zane Grey. He loved *Lord of the Rings* when my husband and I bought it for him, and for years after that we gave him a Tolkien calendar every Christmas.

"Where to?" I ask.

"Oh, maybe the Waterloo Restaurant and some onion soup might be good," he says. "Then let's go to Thornton Street." There are no surprises here, but that doesn't matter anymore. I like the routine.

It's a little cool today—the unpredictable late days of summer have arrived in Ohio. He's checked his outside thermometer and entered the temperature in his journal, so he knows to put on a vinyl coat and zip it up. He doesn't like to see cooler weather approaching, especially winter. His son will give him rules he won't want to follow, but he will so that he can get through the hard months and see his snapdragons and marigolds again, his daffodils (*daf-nails*, he calls them) and his *crocuses croaking*. Paul Jr., the orthopedic surgeon, sometimes wishes his father would start worrying a little more about his bones. But he won't. Uncle Paul only worries about being cooped up. Worries, as my uncle puts it, about *being put under house arrest.*

We drive down Aster toward Waterloo Road and pass the first block of the Aster Avenue business district, where Firestone Park families did their shopping when we were kids.

"That's where Ross McDowell had his dry cleaning business, until just a little while ago," Uncle Paul says, pointing in front of us.

I'm sorry to hear Ross McDowell isn't there anymore.

"Mudder," Uncle Paul adds.

"What?" I ask.

"I used to call him 'Mudder.'"

I think he says "Mother," and I can't figure out what he means. So I ask again.

"*You* know," he says, "like a race horse, a 'mudder.' Ross McDowell went with Sid to Northfield Racetrack come rain or shine. He was lucky in mud, like the race horses that run through it as smooth as brown gravy, ain't wavy. He'd come home all covered in mud, and that was sort of funny for a cleaner, don't you think!"

"Well," I ask, "do you have a name yet for the new guy who took over?"

"Sure," Uncle Paul says. "He's 'New Mudder.' "

"Oh," I say, and smile. *Of course.*

He's hungry, and happy his soup comes right away. He's ordered a piece of cherry pie. He eats it in five bites, washing it down with a loud strong slurp from his cup of coffee (a refill by the time dessert arrives). He never talks while he eats.

I've noticed this about people in my family who struggled through the Depression. My mother and father were silent when they ate, too. There's a fierceness about food in my uncle Paul. There's no leisure between his bites, just anticipation of feeling full. He waits for the server to put his bowl on the table, and holds a spoon in one hand and a fork in the other, both positioned vertically. It's like a race at Northfield Park. Each bite is a furlong. The server doesn't even have time to offer her exit line ("There you go!") before he's forgotten her, forgotten me, and is devoted to that layer of cheese floating on top of his onion soup. He'll scrape every shred from the sides eventually, and tip the tureen into the spoon to drain it of all liquid.

We drive down Grant after lunch, and I tell him what I've found.

"Your grandma must have believed in miracles!" my uncle Paul says after he learns that Anna took August back, apparently with no more than her pastor's assurance that August would behave. I didn't know what my uncle's reaction would be. He's a devout Catholic and doesn't believe in divorce. I thought he might think the story had a happy ending because Grandma and Grandpa got back together again, but I forgot that he was there to witness the unhappy years that followed. Maybe that's what he's thinking about when he mentions Anna and her belief in miracles.

I can tell from his tone that my grandma's decision surprises him. But it doesn't bother him the way it bothers me. He doesn't find as incomprehensible as I do the seven words about Anna's divorce on the court's final journal entry—*The plaintiff dismisses this action without prejudice.*

"Well, that's that," he says when he hears them. He shrugs his shoulders and soon focuses his full attention on Thornton Street.

He doesn't seem to worry much about anything anymore. He treats the mystery of Anna and August's marriage the same way he works a crossword puzzle. If he comes to a block he can't resolve, with some impossible words in it (words he doesn't know, or are gone from memory), he moves on to a different quadrant of the puzzle. And after a while if he can't fill in the blanks, he sets the paper aside and glances at his mountain ash or turns on the TV to catch the score of an Ohio State game. He might come back to the puzzle later in the day. Or he might not.

We arrive at the corner of Thornton and Grant, just north of the post office. Uncle Paul's thoughts are probably with Ruth now, but I'm still thinking about August and Anna Haberkost. This corner was always known as the "Haberkost corner" in the neighborhood, because since the nineteenth century the Haberkosts owned properties close to the intersection. The property that stood on the actual corner belonged to the Crislips. Grandma's house was right next-door, just north of it. The Crislips owned a double cottage—one side their grocery store (Crislips' Grocery Store), the other, the house they lived in.

Crislips' Grocery Store was where I learned how to pick out vegetables and wait for change. It's where I first stared inside a pomegranate Mr. Crislip cut for me. There was always something to do and the chance for pleasure if Grandma let you walk out of the house in the morning with a little money in your hand.

The Crislips always carried brooms, but that never frightened me. They were patient with us kids. It's funny that I can't remember their faces, but I can still see their brooms and their aprons. I think the Crislips were stout people, but I'm not sure about that either. Aprons made people look like all stomach to me, except when Grandma wore

Carol, author, and Paul Jr. in front of Grandma's house, with Crislips' Grocery Store to the left

one. She was slender no matter what she had on. Even an apron couldn't plump up a skeleton.

"You remember Mr. Crislip?" I ask my uncle.

"Oh, sure!" he says. "Good old Crislip."

"Grandma used to sit in the living room and just stare at that store out her south window. Remember?" I say.

"Yep. But it wasn't always Crislips' Grocery Store," Uncle Paul says.

He's surprised me again. Whenever I talk to my cousin Carol about the old neighborhood, we both reminisce about the grocery store. It's one of the touchstones of our common memory. Carol lived

right next to Crislips' for years and years after the Coynes left Goosetown, when she and Marie moved into Grandma's house. We can't
both be wrong about this, especially Carol.

"Carol and I went there almost every day when I lived in Goosetown, Uncle Paul. I'm pretty sure it *always* was a grocery store."

"It was a parsonage."

"No," I tell him. "Our church was up on Voris and Sumner, don't
you remember that? And wasn't the parsonage in Tallmadge when I
was little?" I had a vague memory of its being there.

Uncle Paul kept track of the Lutheran church through his Lutheran wife, since he was Catholic and went to St. Bernard's himself. So I
wonder if maybe he's just confused, or has it wrong. He's the one who
keeps telling me that his memory isn't any good anymore, so I don't
know why he's insisting on this.

"Not always," he says. "Until they built the big church up on Voris and Sumner, Concordia was just around the corner from Grandma's house in that little church that used to be there. And the parsonage for old Concordia was on the corner lot where you remember
Crislips' being."

There's no use saying more.

After I drop Uncle Paul off, I hurry home and find my mother's
folder marked "Concordia." She saved everything about her church,
including programs and pamphlets from anniversary celebrations. It
was one of the most important things in her life, as it was in the lives of
most of the Haberkost women. After she developed Alzheimer's, my
father, a fallen Catholic, accompanied her to Concordia every Sunday.
It was the last place she recognized, along with her hairdresser's shop.

I discover what should no longer surprise me: Uncle Paul is right.
There's a page in the Fiftieth Anniversary booklet showing the first
Concordia Church on Thornton Street and then the second Concor-
dia built twenty years later on Sumner and Voris. I knew there was a

church on Thornton, right around the corner from Grandma's house, but I never realized it had once been our family's church. It was the Slovak Lutheran Church when I was young, where Eddie and I learned about hell. The pamphlet explained the church on Thornton had been built in 1905 to house Concordia Lutheran, with a membership of forty. By 1927 the congregation had grown to five hundred members and relocated to the new church up the street. The original building had been sold, probably to the Slovak Lutheran Church.

Shortly after Concordia moved, the parsonage moved too. Moved to the Tallmadge location I remember. The pastor had bought a piece of wild land earlier in his career, seven miles from the church, and his parishioners had built a house on it for him.

For the first twenty years of her marriage, Anna Haberkost saw a parsonage out her south window. Out her west window, in her kitchen, she saw a corner of a church. *Her* church.

I begin to sense how strongly our stories are connected to the buildings we look at out the windows of our houses. I had forgotten the lesson of the new post office. Neither Uncle Paul nor I see it there. We see old Thornton Park. It was the same lesson of the building on the corner of Cross and Grant—Grandpa saw a bar; Eddie and I, a drugstore; someone today would see the Bottoms Up Lounge. Each remembered version would fire minds and memories differently, affecting perception in profound ways.

Grandma saw God, and God's minister, when she looked out the south and west windows of her home. Those were *her* windows, the windows in the living room and the windows in the kitchen—the places where she labored to feed her children and wore herself out tallying all their needs. The places where she hid from Grandpa.

I saw only pomegranates in Crislips' Grocery Store.

We stare through our windows a hundred times a day to get our bearing. There's no more telling reflecting pool than a window. Our own image merges with the image on the other side of the glass, and for an instant they are the same.

I've lived by a funeral home for the past ten years, and it steals my attention. I watch people stand in the parking lot in black suits, sometimes crying, sometimes smoking cigarettes. I see the funeral director sweep the porch and greet florists who drop off arrangements at the door. The Greek Revival house where the dead in our town come is the first thing I see every morning as I open the shutters of my study window before I start to write. I read obituaries and visit the dead more often than I did before I bought this house. The dead are my neighbors now. The thin pane of window glass in my study is the only thing between us.

There is a fence that divides our properties, but from the second floor where my study is, it does no good. It's not high enough to hide the funeral home. Late on snowy nights, at 3:00 A.M., a snow plow comes to clear the parking lot, and I hear its noise. Even at night, in the dark, I'm reminded that a funeral home is there. Sometimes I become angry that I'm losing sleep listening to the "beep, beep, beep" of the plow and think about calling the director to complain.

Grandma lived right beside God. She was devout, and it might have brought her comfort to know that all she had to do was open her drapes to see the emblems of her faith. Even after Mr. Crislip moved into the neighborhood and the church relocated a few blocks south, Grandma must have seen the buildings the way they were before. She saw religion everywhere. When Mr. Crislip exited his store dressed in his great white apron at the end of a day to retire to his cottage for the night, she might have mistaken him for her pastor on Easter morning, robed in white.

It would have taken no more than a minute for the pastor to walk out the door of his parsonage in 1926, up Anna's steps, and propose his plan for August's release and redemption. They might have had tea or coffee in the kitchen. Anna loved coffee. She probably loved the minister, too. He was gentler than August and talked to her. It was so close to Christmas! There might have been soft snow pressed against the window they were looking through, framing the little white church, and the picture would have been irresistible. Perhaps the pastor said he would cut a tree for her and help her put it up. She let down her guard. Coffee, a few kind words, and the pastor's promise might have been enough to convince Anna to let August come home. Enough to seal it. She might not have known that the pastor would soon move away, and imagined how nice it would be to have him come to her house more often than he normally did. He was such a busy man. But he would be August's guardian, if she agreed. I see him sitting there sipping his coffee, promising her a different man when August returned. A better husband. A kinder father to her children. The pastor would help her through this. He would help them *both*. He would watch August and reprimand him, if he needed to. The pastor, and God, wanted the marriage to work.

If he brought God into it, Anna would have known she had no choice. If God wanted her to take August back, how could she say *no*? She could say *no* to August, perhaps even to the pastor, but not to God.

Her own family was building the new church, every brick and beam. How could she say *no* at a time like this?

Uncle Paul was right. Anna believed in miracles. She said yes to her pastor, and yes to the hope her church had in her. And in doing so, I'm sure she thought she said yes to God. She could mend this union—salvage it—and an institution named *Concordia* would show her how to rid her life of its unbearable discord. The Grant Street house would become a cathedral that emitted only harmonious sounds into the neighborhood, the voices of Anna and August and all their children joining gleefully in song.

It was nearly Christmas, the time when stories of redemption came true.

Anna loved and feared the church much more than she ever did August Haberkost. The real authority in her life was never August. He was just a nuisance, though sometimes a very brutal one. The true authority was her religion. She must have thought that somehow she could learn how to love August again if she opened her heart to the lessons of a great institution and a great pastor. She needed to believe in a miracle. Manna from heaven, the flaming bush, water to wine, deliverance from a furnace of fire, Jonah in the belly of a fish. August sober and kind. *Voilà!*

She trusted the pastor, but he moved away. She couldn't shout for help any longer, so she retreated into prayer. Took a vow of silence.

When I looked at the journal entry that brought Anna's petition for divorce to a close, its dark edges seemed to frame the words written on a single line. The page could have been a piece of window glass. Those words, in fact, might have been etched on the windows that faced the church and the parsonage. *Plaintiff dismisses this action without prejudice.*

The words on the document from the Court of Common Pleas were inevitable. A kindly pastor and friend, a sweet white church in her backyard (and the imminent prospect of a huge Gothic church built brick by brick by the hands of her own family), the creeds and hymns and prayers that were her daily recitations—these were forces of great consequence in Anna's life. If she had ripped them away, rejected or betrayed them, she may have found little of herself that was recognizable.

So Anna dismissed her motion and, *without prejudice*, walked into the remaining chapters of her life. Before she would know it, she would rest under a single stone with August Haberkost. For eternity.

CHAPTER 26

Scotty, Aunt Marie's husband, knows something about the day August disappeared. We're sitting at his kitchen table playing with his cats.

He has no recollection of Anna's petition for divorce, though. He could not have known about it directly, since Scotty didn't meet my aunt Marie until the 1940s, long after Anna filed her petition. And indirectly? I don't think Marie would have said anything to Scotty about it because there is no evidence the Haberkost children were ever told. Even if they had been, they would have thought it was something from so long ago that it hardly bore mentioning. Haberkosts don't dwell on things like that. They live practically. In the present.

I don't know why I can't too.

What Scotty knows is that August's son took him away. Put him in a car, and drove it down Grant Street and out of town.

I don't know what to make of this, so I laugh and exaggerate the story. "Was he kidnapped by his own son!"

Scotty laughs too, but he says about the same thing Uncle Paul has told me. Grandpa was "up to his old stuff." He doesn't elaborate, but he says that August brought the wrath of his family down on him and caused his son to materialize off a Navy ship. His oldest son had left home the first chance he could and joined the Navy, but now he was back.

The agent of Anna's miracle had arrived in the form of the son August had threatened to kill. He performed the miracle the pastor had promised her over twenty-five years before. August wouldn't bother her anymore. This time he would be permanently banished from his home. Even after he returned to Akron to be buried, his hearse would go directly to the Eckard-Baldwin Funeral Home and not pass by the Grant Street house. He'd never be near it again, alive or dead.

"Where did Howard take him, Scotty?" I ask.

"Don't know," he says.

But he has a clue.

"One night," Scotty says, "we were driving late and Marie fell into a light sleep. She woke up (we'd stopped at a traffic light) and saw a stone building in front of her. It was just an elementary school, but one of those old, high ones that look more like dark castles than schools. She screamed, 'Don't take me there! Please, no!'"

Scotty says this wasn't the first time she'd dreamed about a stone building and woke afraid. "It was in all her nightmares," he tells me, just before he shoos the cats out the screen door.

"What building was it?" I ask.

"She once saw the place where August went," he says. "My guess is that's the building that she dreamed about. I don't know how she got there, though. She never drove. Never had a license. No one else in the family ever went, as far as I know."

If any of the Haberkost children would have made the trip to see their exiled father, it would have been Aunt Marie. She was the one who loved family history and always liked to be on top of all the gossip.

"Did she visit him?" I ask Scotty.

"Don't think so," he says. "Just looked at the place. Drove by it. She said there were horses and buggies, like she'd traveled back in time."

"Sounds strange," I say. "Maybe that was just part of the dream."

"My guess is it's Holmes County. Buggies? Amish country."

After I leave Scotty, I call my uncle Paul to see if he wants to help me search for a stone building somewhere in Holmes County. I try to lure him with the promise of a piece of pecan pie at a good Amish restaurant down that way, but he's made plans to eat at Swenson's with Cuz tomorrow. He loves Swenson's cheeseburgers (another Akron specialty), so I'm on my own.

CHAPTER 27

I wake early and begin the drive to the Holmes County Courthouse in Millersburg, sixty-five miles south of Goosetown. The land
quickly becomes hillier. More rural. The rich Ohio farmland of everyone's imagination. Barns and dairy cows and vast fields of corn,
along with Appalachian foothills that somehow seem disorienting. I
pass a sign for Hotel Millersburg and then some for Amish country. A
Millersburg Corporation sign welcomes me. Then one for a hospital
zone. I spill down a hill and come to a Y in the road at Washington
and Clay. I go on and soon reach the Holmes County Courthouse.

A quick discovery. August's death certificate.

His last residence is listed: Castle Nursing Home, Millersburg,
Ohio.

On the way to the courthouse I'd stopped at Apple Creek, a former mental asylum in Wayne County. I was sure that's where Grandpa had been hauled. It went along with the dramatic story I was inventing of a powerful son returning from the Navy in full uniform to
capture his crazy father and rescue his mom. But I'd been wrong. August hadn't gone mad after all. At least, not legally. His name wasn't
on any of the old ledger sheets authorities let me look through, though
they said there might be lost pages.

I learn from a courthouse clerk that the original nursing home is
still standing, but it's abandoned now.

I find the ruin and walk around it. Built like a castle high on a lonely hill, it reminds me of the old city jail in Akron—where Grandpa had resided earlier. There's a turret in the center, and iron grates on the bottom halves of the windows. I read a notice about its fate taped to a windowpane. The building is a warehouse now, it says, but scheduled for demolition. Soon, a wrecking ball will fell this massive structure, and then two castles will be lost to me.

Some of the stone from the walls is chipping off. In the back, I find a pile of old chairs, discarded objects, and a NO DUMPING sign. The wrought iron railing that must have been there when my grandpa arrived has grown scales of rust. Remnants of an old brick patio poke through debris, and concrete blocks have been placed at the edge to contain it.

I drive across the street to the corporate offices of the new Castle Nursing Home. There I meet a very elderly nurse who worked for Castle in the early days. I tell her I'm trying to find out what happened to my grandpa. She talks about Castle Nursing Home in the 1950s—Grandpa's years. She had been in charge of the men's ward. The news is unbelievable.

Castle took mild mental patients then, she says, though mental illness wasn't really understood. A patient's behavior was the only thing they went on. No one knew anything about the brain.

"Patients sometimes transferred here from Apple Creek. I don't know if your grandpa was one of them." I tell her I'd stopped there earlier, and found no record that he'd ever lived at Apple Creek.

"When they arrived," she says, "they cried about shock treatments, being strapped down, huge doses of Thorazine and Compazine. Even here we used restraints, especially when patients were belligerent. It's all we could do." She pauses and shakes her head. "Alcoholics and schizophrenics and the demented were all lodged together. Treated the same. But things aren't like that anymore."

She asks me if I'd been over to the castle. I nod.

"That's where the men's ward was. In that turret," she says. "That's where your grandpa would have been."

"Did you by any chance nurse my grandpa?" I ask her.

"What did he look like?" she says.

"I have a picture of him," I say. "He was a large man with brilliant white hair, and he always wore a white shirt. He may have spoken German." I show her the photograph I'd brought along. I had placed it safely in the pocket window of my wallet, along with pictures of my husband and my son.

She looks at it, then back at me. I want her to remember. I want her, even, to lie. But her eyes won't allow her to.

"I don't recall him," she says. "I took care of so many people."

She doesn't want to talk about those early years anymore. I can tell. She's very nice, but she doesn't want to think about my grandpa Haberkost or the men's ward of old Castle Nursing Home. She's my uncle's generation, and she's tired out.

"I've tried to forget their faces," she says, and I know she wants me to stop asking questions.

She looks at the death certificate I hand her before she leaves for her shift.

"Alzheimer's," she says. "That's what your grandpa had."

The immediate cause of death listed on his death certificate is "viral infection," probably pneumonia. I haven't looked beyond my quick conclusion that pneumonia took the old man. But there's something else. Secondary conditions include "arteriosclerotic heart disease" and "senility." The old nurse can read the code for Alzheimer's. And so can I, now that I see it there. *Senility* and *hardening of the arteries* were often shorthand in the 1950s for what the medical profession would soon begin to label Alzheimer's disease.

I had come in search of some great drama. A grandfather who was criminally insane and had lived out his life in a loony bin, laced in a straitjacket. As I rode toward Millersburg, I had grown excited by the idea that he was insane. That Akron couldn't contain his madness, so he'd been carted away. *They're coming to take me away, Ha Ha! To the happy home, with trees and flowers and chirping birds, and basket weavers who sit and smile and twiddle their thumbs and toes.* Old campfire songs I'd sung in the dark woods beneath a full moon kept coming back as I drove farther and farther down Route 83 toward Apple Creek.

Instead, I've found a sick man with Alzheimer's living in a nursing home in Millersburg with other old people, and I really hadn't planned on that.

I never wanted Goosetown to be about *Alzheimer's*. Because if it's about Alzheimer's, it's about me.

August and Anna had seven children. Four lived into their seventies and eighties, and they all developed Alzheimer's disease. Terrible, profound cases of it. I saw them die. I took care of some of them. I saw my mother's mind evanesce right in front of me. I saw fury in her eyes, felt it in her fists, heard it in ugly words she had never used before. I watched the calmest woman I'd ever known turn into a beast.

Turn into her father.

I'm closer to finding an answer to August's disappearance. At least now I know some of the things that might have complicated that last terrible scene at home. His alcoholism probably flared up again, causing Anna to summon her son. But his behavior might have been intensified because of the onset of his illness. Maybe he wasn't just violent anymore, but violent *and* sick. His wildness, connected to alcohol, returned, but it was more explosive this time because tangles and plaques were knotting his brain. In the early 1950s, my family had only the words that were available to them. They named my grand-pa's behavior *drunkenness* or called him *son-of-a-bitch,* but neither label was quite right.

Earlier scenes in his life, though, seem less complicated. He had accumulated a ledger full of offenses. He was no saint. All the Seven Deadly Sins were his. They had led to the acts recorded and pre-served in Akron history. Stealing and Pawning a Watch. Breaking and Entering. Threatening to Kill His Son.

I add one more item to the list.

Passing on his DNA.

CHAPTER 28

"Poor old guy," Uncle Paul says when I tell him about Grandpa living in that turret for nine years, surrendering a little of his brain each day to the scalpel of the disease that killed so many Haberkosts, and also killed Edith, Uncle Paul's second wife.

This is just like Uncle Paul. He finds out someone has suffered, and then forgives them for everything that went before. He should have been a priest. I asked him once if he'd ever considered it. He said the priest at St. Bernard's wanted him to be an altar boy, but he wouldn't agree to it. *I want to sing!* he told the priest. And that's what he did his whole life. Barbershop music, mainly.

He's gone too far this time with his charity, though.

"Grandma testified that he threatened to kill Howard, Uncle Paul!" I say to him.

"He was sick," he says.

I *know* I have to consider how Grandpa's illness affected the way he behaved, and I have. I tell Uncle Paul my interpretation of the kidnap scene. I've already acknowledged that my grandpa may have been sick when they took him to Millersburg. It probably played a part.

I've even tried to imagine August in the throes of the disease. After all, I nursed August's daughter. It's not something that I'm incapable of imagining.

When I try to picture my grandpa lodged in that turret in Millersburg, I think of Annabelle, just as mad, sitting under a skylight in her own bright wing of a state-of-the-art Alzheimer's unit. Neither of them knew where they were. Or, by the end, had any concept of *where* at all.

And I also think of the future of my cousins and me. This disease, so strong in our family, isn't going to skip our generation. My cousins and I are in our fifties, and it won't be long before Alzheimer's will come for some of us. Maybe all. I'm doing everything I can to delay it. I hope, to prevent it. I take vitamins, eat well, stay as fit as I can, drink the right juices, avoid all cholesterol, scour the results of new clinical studies, and read and write all day long to keep my mind awake. Sometimes I feel I've been so careful with my brain that it will never turn on me, but I know that's the height of arrogance. Why should I be spared?

I'm August's granddaughter. A direct descendant.

I carry his genes.

I'm fooling myself if I think I'm someone else.

I tell some of this to Uncle Paul, but he still looks at me funny. It's as if what I've said isn't enough. He thinks I'm not compassionate, and he's disappointed. I can tell. He won't say it, but it's in his eyes.

He's probably right. A part of me does hate, or fear, August Haberkost. I don't want to get too close to him and have no desire to embrace my progenitor. Grandpa was not easy for his family to live with, and probably not a very good man. I pity my grandma for her life with him. It's hard to feel as sorry for her as I do without blaming him. I don't know how to be as kind as Uncle Paul.

And how can I disperse the gloomy shadow this man casts over the Haberkosts of my generation? Over me? How can I dispel this matter of DNA? I know it's irrational to blame him. Someone had the gene long before August inherited it. But I still feel the same way about him as I do the Tin-Can Frisbee Man of my Goosetown years, or the wicked boy who frightened Eddie and me outside the church on Thornton Street. August is mortality—just the way that they were— and I don't care to shake his hand. He's standing over me, reeking of beer and failure, and grinning through yellow teeth. *You are me, little girl. And I am you,* I hear him say.

He's after me. I'm three years old again and begin to run, and call him names.

Connected to that gene is a fear almost as great as death itself: the fear of losing language. Watching words vanish one by one, the way my mother did. Maybe that's another reason I cherish Anna's testimony as much as I do.

For Annabelle, flies became birds; shoes, hats; love, suspicion. Her brain flat-lined and she stopped talking. She just sat, like a stone monument in front of a library. Or a lion in front of a courthouse. A world of words all behind her, all incomprehensible. She couldn't dress or speak, and then she couldn't swallow or eat. Her breasts, hair, and eyes grew flat, too. One day, she slid from the room through a crack and disappeared. I never saw the woman I knew again. It was different from Grandpa's disappearance, because my mother was still in the room with me.

And that's how it was for her sisters Helen, Marie, and Betty. All those women, dead from the same gene. Four of the five sisters. Ruth, who died at sixty, was the only daughter spared. *Spared* by breast cancer.

Maybe it's not just anger my uncle is asking me to shed. He won't stop staring in my direction, so it's probably something else.

Maybe it's my arrogance. Can I really pretend to know when and where a disease like Alzheimer's begins? I've imagined it erupting in the final scenes in the Grant Street house. But maybe it began sooner. Is that what my uncle means when he excuses everything?

Do I really know when Grandpa's first symptoms appeared, or what they were? My mother behaved oddly years before she was diagnosed—decades. *Not like herself today*, my dad and I used to say, and then we'd laugh uncomfortably and talk about something else. It was just some little thing that she did, or said, but odd enough for us to notice it. There were moments before clear onset when I felt there was a stranger in the room with me when Annabelle and I were alone. Her powder blue eyes were too light sometimes, too still, almost stiff, as if a great white emptiness lay behind them and was pushing out. And what of her acute nervousness at the sound of a crying child, something she experienced before she was forty years old? Could that have been related to the bizarre circuitry in her brain? My uncle called it "Having One Ovary," but if he'd had a word like *Alzheimer's* back then, he might have used it instead.

Do we acquire a disease such as this as we age, or is it always there, resting in some recess of the brain, waking up in little spurts until in one huge yawn it devours everything? Devours *us*?

So how do I know when August first became "sick," to use my uncle's word?

When August brought the wrath of his family down on him—*all* the times in his life, perhaps not just in that final scene—could it have been his disease at work?

There, Uncle Paul. I still don't feel your tenderness toward the man, but you can lower your eyebrow some.

CHAPTER 29

When I saw my grandpa's death certificate, I knew I would finish this book. It wasn't because I'd finally found out what happened to August and I had an ending for my story. It had nothing to do with that.

Before seeing that document, I had tampered with the evidence. The evidence of my own life, I mean. I'd deceived myself so many times. I'd told myself that my mother's illness was an aberration, and that her sisters had small strokes that led to different versions of dementia than hers. I had looked for studies and articles that diminished the role of heredity in the disease and passed on the results to my family.

I spoke to support groups whenever they called and asked. I was positive and hopeful.

But Alzheimer's is a force that's *very* real now. And very close. Knowing that it might be rushing toward me, or I toward it, how can I choose not to speak?

I no longer have an option.

If memory and language might soon disappear, how can I take the job of recovering my first five years so lightly?

And what possible benefit has silence ever brought me? What benefit did it bring Anna Haberkost?

My grandmother would have been lost to me if she hadn't spoken up. I have to remember this.

How do I know when the first sign will appear? Maybe it already has.

Quick.

Who is the President of the United States?

What is today's date?

Repeat these words: HOUSE, BLUEBIRD, TREE.

Spell "WORLD" backwards.

Draw a clock at 6:15.

What are the three words I asked you to repeat?

Say them now.

CHAPTER 30

I'm in the courthouse again, looking at an old police report. I can't stop my Goosetown search, and this time I haven't even called my uncle Paul so he could make some excuse not to ride along. The report isn't about August, but Eddie. It's the accident report from the day he died. The day he was run over at the corner of Cross and Grant. I've never had the courage to inquire about his death before today, but here I am reading descriptions by the officers at the scene and a statement by the driver, who was interviewed. Here I am studying two little drawings of Eddie on the ground that the officers sketched on site with lead pencils.

A young German man—a Goosetown man—drove the car that killed my cousin. He wasn't going fast. Just twenty-five. He was a DP, a displaced person from the War, and had just arrived in town, along with eight hundred other refugees. He was a Catholic man driving home to his family, starting a new life in a new country. He wasn't speeding, he wasn't drinking. He was just going home.

The officers called to the scene measured ninety feet of skid marks up to the point of impact. The driver had tried to stop. The first drawing at the accident site shows a tiny stick figure of Eddie lying flat, spread on the street east to west.

The second drawing shows him under the car, forty-eight feet from the point of impact. You can see only the head and a little of a shoulder.

The driver who killed Eddie said he saw the little girl and the little boy running across the street, but they came so fast he couldn't stop. The right fender of his car knocked Eddie to the ground and dragged him down the street. Everything stopped right in front of the Quality Tool and Machine Shop.

The '49 Olds has huge broad front fenders. The emblem on the nose of that model is a world wrapped in steel. That image would have been the last thing Eddie saw.

Eddie was a victim of Rubber Town and industry and a century gone mad. He was a boy from the Rubber Capital of the World killed by a tire. He wasn't the first Haberkost to fall victim to speed and asphalt and rubber tires. Haberkosts, and Haberkost children, had been hurt before on Akron streets. There are stories in the *Beacon*.

John, one of the original Haberkost brothers who emigrated from Germany, was run down by a Nypano fast freight train. His right foot caught under the wheels of the engine and was *crushed to pulp*, a story says.

The bad luck of the original Haberkost brothers continued to their children. In 1890, Frederick's son Christian, just a boy, drove a delivery wagon for G. G. Auger, a Thornton Street grocer. His horse became frightened by the dairy cows being driven down East South Street, plunged forward, knocked down a cow, breaking its horn, and threw Christian onto the hard ground. In 1906, Dorothy (Dora) Haberkost, age nine, and Clara Haberkost, age seventeen, children of Patrolman August J. Haberkost, were both struck by a Canton–Akron car of the NOTL (Northern Ohio Traction and Light) company at the intersection of Brown and East Market. They were out riding in a pony cart, turned onto Market, failed to see the streetcar going east, and were hit. Clara was thrown onto the ground and badly bruised. Dora lost two teeth. They were taken to the hospital, but were among the lucky children who got to leave. They were both sent home the same afternoon.

Anna with her children the day of Eddie's funeral

Even children in my mother's generation were injured or killed on the streets of Akron. Bobby K., born in 1919, the grandson of Christian, died at age eleven. He was a student at Akron's Oak Grove School, on the corner of Bellows and Archwood, and was killed by a truck when he, like Eddie, tried to cross a street.

But it isn't just the details of Eddie's accident—or the accidents of other Haberkosts—that I'm looking for. I want to know how Eddie's sister, Carol, and Grandma survived a thing like that. And how would I? How *have* I?

CHAPTER 31

Carol and I are sitting in the basement of the old Polsky Building in downtown Akron, across from the police department where Carol works. I want to buy her a sandwich or a Coke, but she doesn't want a thing.

I've never talked to her about Eddie. Never once. I never asked her what happened after the ambulance came. Until now, I really didn't want to have this conversation with her. She contracted polio the autumn after Eddie died. People always said her immunity had been lowered by the stress of her brother's death. From what we know now about the role of stress in our lives, this may have been true. Since she's gotten older, she's showing signs of post–polio syndrome— bones always hurting her, muscles weak, fatigue. There's no way to repair the bones in her bad leg anymore. She'll have to retire soon.

I gently tell her I want to know what happened that day.

Carol begins to talk. She says she reached the other side of Grant and turned to find Eddie, but he was gone.

Her next memory is of a neighbor throwing a blanket over her and quickly walking her home to Grandma's house, trying to make sure the car that struck Eddie was out of the little girl's view. But Carol had already seen her brother under a wheel.

The neighbor told Grandma the story as best she could, Carol said, then hurried away.

"Was there any blood?" That's what Carol remembers Grandma asking her.

"No," Carol said, because there had been none that the little girl could see.

"Then it will be all right," Grandma kept saying. Holding and rocking Carol, she said again and again it would be all right.

"Grandma believed that if no blood was spilled, there was nothing wrong with you inside," Carol says.

I wish she'd stop now, but Carol says it one more time.

"Was there any blood?" Carol would scream "No!" and cry and then Anna would ask again.

"No, Grandma! No blood!"

I'm startled by my grandma's words, and by the courage it must take for my cousin to say them.

She leaves for work, and I cross the street to the John D. Morley Health Center where death certificates are stored for residents of Summit County.

Cerebral vascular occlusion. Those are the final words about Anna, written on the last official document she would leave behind in this town. And what were the words on Eddie's certificate? *Head, chest, and internal injuries*.

Blood was on the loose in both of them.

CHAPTER 32

In the evening after my meeting with Carol, I begin to think. I think about what Carol has told me. Told me about poor Eddie, whose days were so few that a kindergartener could count them.

I think about Carol and Marie and Anna and the rest of our family trying to find a way to live without Eddie.

The Coynes' answer was to flee Goosetown, and never come back.

But I don't think there's really any way to find peace after a loss like that. You can't run away, there's nowhere to hide. And you can't forget.

I often think that Carol became a police dispatcher so she could return every day to the accident scene. Although I'm sure she'd deny this, isn't it possible that she chose her career so that she could watch out for children all her life and try to keep them safe by dispatching police to accident sites? Isn't it possible that part of her knew this was the closest she could ever come to getting Eddie back? Each time she dispatched an officer, she rescued her brother again.

Grandma, as far as I can tell, did exactly what she always did when life became unbearable: She grew more and more still. Then, she completely petrified. Six years after Eddie died, her arteries turned to stone and she suffered a fatal stroke.

But Grandma was hemorrhaging long before a blood vessel burst inside her head, and this is what Carol has taught me to see. Anna just didn't know it, the way she didn't know that Eddie was bleeding inside. I don't mean this literally, of course. It wasn't blood, at first, that Grandma kept inside. It was *words*. After August came back from jail, and then Eddie died, Anna grew more and more silent. Words are always bloody, and as Anna grew more still, anger and grief swelled inside of her like a bloody stream. One day, it burst.

Grandma didn't know how deadly it was to have so many secrets. Or, she had forgotten. Only on one glorious November day in 1926 did she ever really speak, and release the blood. By December 22, 1926, when she agreed to take August back, the blood was dangerously building up again. When Eddie died, I think she constructed a veritable dam inside herself. In a much, much smaller way, it's what I did with the secret of the devil fish after Eddie disappeared. And what I've done so often after that.

Words held inside can be as fatal as internal hemorrhaging.

That's what Anna didn't fully understand, though something in her must have sensed it that November day.

Anna's fondness for bloodless silence forces me to look hard at my own life. At what I've kept inside that might be killing me. At all the things I've lacked the courage to put on the page. There have been so many secrets since the devil fish. I don't lie, exactly, but I keep things hidden. Is there really any difference between the two?

When I wrote *In a Tangled Wood*, the story of my mother's battle with Alzheimer's, I didn't tell about my failure to go with her to the crematorium. I didn't tell that I wasn't in the room when my father died, when I wrote about him. And I don't always write about the living, even though they're deeply on my mind. I'm more comfortable writing about the dead because they can't come after me. I have a chronic illness, but I've never written about it. Sometimes doctors who read my work guess what it is, because they recognize the code I use. Once, in act 3 of my own life, I almost stepped over the steep edge of despair, but pulled myself back in time. (I still don't have the courage to talk about this.) There have been terrible shocks in my life that I've got to get down, but I can't. And horrible disappointments. And that's just the beginning of what I haven't said.

It's a Haberkost tendency to keep things in. I have no idea what damage my secrets have already done to me.

My grandparents were both thieves.

And I'm a thief too: I sometimes steal the truth because I lack the courage to tell it.

The truth, the whole truth, and nothing but the bloody truth, please.

CHAPTER 33

Paul Jr. calls me one evening in early fall. I'm alarmed, even before he gives me any news. He usually calls around Christmas to set up a holiday dinner with my husband and me, but it's a little too soon for that. It's September, and the leaves have just started to turn.

I've been neglecting Uncle Paul, with the start of school. It's such a busy time for me. I haven't seen him for several weeks, so I'm worried when I hear my cousin's voice.

"It's Dad," he says, and I inhale the words, "What's wrong?"

"He broke his hip," Paul says, giving none of the details and avoiding the medical terms that come so naturally to him, the Bone Man.

"How?!" I ask, knowing there hasn't even been snow yet. I'm secretly relieved it's just his hip, and not a fatal heart attack.

"He was invited to play cards by the neighbors and lost his footing. Slipped on a back step coming out of his house."

"Oh, no," I say. I ask Paul for his father's room number at St. Thomas Hospital (it's the Catholic Hospital in town), and then we both hang up.

Visiting hours are over, so I go the next day. Uncle Paul is outfitted in an oxygen mask, and I don't like his color, but he's alert and seems really happy to see me.

"Babe!" he says. I kiss him. The mask starts to steam.

I look at the huge cast on his leg. They've decided to set the break, though everyone knows at his age this is a risk. Uncle Paul would never have a chance to walk again without the operation, though. It's just that his lungs, that heart—there's only so much a body can bear.

He whispers that the Akron chapter of his Barbershop chorus serenaded him the night before. He's in intensive care, "so they had to get a special dispensation from the Pope to do it," my uncle says, but the joke wears him out. He grows very still.

His breathing is labored. I tell him to rest. I sit beside his bed holding his blue hand, and he's asleep in five seconds. He always could do that. I wish I knew how.

Right before I leave, he pops awake with tears in his eyes. "Don't let them take me to a rest home, Babe!"

"If you need to rest, you'll rest at *my* house, or Paul's!" I tell Uncle Paul. I tell him that the cast is temporary and that we'll be dancing soon. "Gosh, I really love you!" I tell him.

I call my cousin later and ask if he knows any more about Uncle Paul's condition. He says he has a shot. It's going to be hard—the surgery was tough on the old guy—but he just might make his next birthday after all.

His ninetieth.

CHAPTER 34

A day later, my cousin calls again. "You better come in tonight if you want to see Dad, Joyce."

"What?" I say.

"Pneumonia. We were afraid of that. He's not responding to the drugs."

His heart's going to give out after all. I can't believe it.

I race to his room, and he's nearly comatose. But he opens his eyes once, and smiles at my husband and me. And then he starts breathing that slow way the dying have. Small breaths between long pauses. Then longer still.

The nurse tells me there hasn't been any change, his vitals are stable, and he'll last the night.

"Go ahead and leave," she says.

It's late, I'm tired, and I make the mistake of listening to her. The hard lessons of Goosetown still haven't sunk in.

I'm not in the room when he dies.

How many more chances do I have to get this right? I wasn't in the room when my mother died, my father, my grandparents, my aunts and uncles, a close friend. And I will never forget the decades of regret my uncle said he felt because he wasn't in the room with Ruth when she died. Death doesn't walk into a room very often. You have to stay and wait for him, and that's a lesson I seem unable to learn.

It's just so much easier to run away.

CHAPTER 35

There are sixty men standing beside his coffin in the Dunn-Quigley Ciriello & Carr Funeral Home on Grant Street. They parade in and form three long rows that tip toward Uncle Paul, waves of gray and black and navy blue. Some of them have known him for the full fifty years he's sung in the Akron Barbershop Chorus.

Under a glass chandelier the conductor steps forward, clears his throat, and talks to the visitors sitting on rows of folding chairs.

"We've come to honor Dad," he says. Everyone in the chorus calls my uncle "Dad."

They sing "I Believe" and my eyes close and I'm sitting in a banquet room somewhere in Akron after the annual Barbershop show. I'm eight years old. Maybe nine. The first event I ever attended that ran past midnight was the Afterglow, a party and singing fest that followed the public concert at Loew's, an Italian Renaissance theater with griffins and a ceiling made of stars. There are cold cuts and pickles and potato salad and red Jell-O and white sheet cake in the room. There are paper flags on each table stuck into cupcakes, and patriotic napkins, and red, white, and blue sequins on lapels. I try to stay awake, but my head hits my uncle's shoulder, and I'm gone.

"Breathe for a minute," the conductor tells his group after they finish the song and he sees them tilting farther toward the casket. Fat men with mustaches hold one another's hands, and younger men stand alone, too thin yet to recognize the comfort of a big man's flesh.

"'The Lord's Prayer,' for Dad," he says, and the men inhale flowers and pink light and death, and begin to sing.

I know it's silly, but whenever I hear that song in church or a funeral home, I lose control, and I don't feel like doing that right now. I try to think of other things. I think of the colored water Aunt Ruth kept in bottles on the windowsill, the rhubarb my uncle grew in his backyard, the driveway he shared with the people next door, the dog he loved that died just weeks before my uncle's fatal fall, the air conditioner he bought me to help battle the fevers of my disease the hot summer after Aunt Ruth died, the way he tap danced in a home movie with my young son riding on his shoulder. But when there are sixty voices in a small room sending words about *the kingdom and the power and the glory* trembling into the air until the glass shakes in the chandelier, it's difficult to find an image strong enough to shut it out.

The "Amen" brings me back into the room.

Then one last song.

"'O Shine on Me' was Dad's favorite," the conductor says. "He always sang the last line alone. It was *his*. Tonight we'll stop the song a little short."

"Will the light in the lighthouse shine on me?" The chorus ends on a question.

Air stops spilling from the fan blades and the room is still. There is no one to sing the final line.

Then someone says, "I can hear him!"

"I can hear him too!" more men say.

There's air again, and the room feels cool. In the false light, all of us can hear Dad's pure bass voice.

Oh, Lordy, how the moon do shine down on these bones, bones, bones, bones of mine!

CHAPTER 36

The morning of the funeral, I dress in black, a simple suit with a mid-calf skirt. I'm going to be a pallbearer for my uncle Paul. My cousin asked me the night before at visiting hours.

I said yes, I'd carry him. But even as I spoke the words, I thought about my clumsiness, my lack of strength. I looked at the coffin the way you look at luggage before you take a long trip, hoping that it will be light enough to bear. The coffin looked like metal, but when I tapped my fingernails on the sides, I was sure it was wood. I hoped it was walnut. I couldn't help thinking that Uncle Paul would love being buried in a walnut box. Then I thought about my uncle's weight. Would he still weigh 180 pounds—even dead?

Now, on this balmy, rainy morning, I'm listening to the funeral director tell all the people who will carry Uncle Paul that it's time and we should position ourselves beside a handle on either side of the closed casket and prepare to lift. My anxiety is even worse than I expected. The box looks as heavy as a ship. Too much for me. I wonder why we can't just put our dead in real boats and set everything aflame, like the Vikings did. Just be done with it, instead of cart it all around.

Our first job is to carry the casket to the hearse for its trip to Sacred Heart of Jesus. That's the church on Grant Street Uncle Paul has attended for several years now, since he stopped driving and had to go with Cuz to her church for mass. We're given short, clipped orders. "Turn to the side," "Grab your handle," "Now lift."

It's even heavier than I had imagined. There's so much inside, and I have all the middle weight. I have the folded hands over his heart, the blue print tie, the stomach, the broken hip. It feels as if I also have the cast, though I know it was probably removed in the embalming room.

Why did he have to go play cards on a September night? Why did he have to lose his footing on a step? A *step*! He'd walked through so much trouble in his life, and gotten by, how could a single step be the thing that tripped him up? A *familiar* step that led up to his own back door?

We lift him a second time up the steep stairs of the church. Bracing my arm, squeezing my hand the way I do in the doctor's office to plump a vein for blood, I grab the handle and feel my feet begin to give. I tighten the muscles in my legs (hoping my calves don't cramp) until the signal reaches my ankles and they remember they are bone—they remember what to do—and rise back up. I feel my shoes right themselves, and my flat heels hit the stone of the first step, then the second. I swear I feel Uncle Paul roll over and turn right toward me as a I climb, because the weight intensifies. Then the third, the fourth, the fifth step, until we are at the top by the church door and I'm out of breath. The muscles in my arms are burning and my joints seem soldered now.

There's more weight than I thought there ever could have been when I sized him up the night before. No one except the staff was in the parlor of the funeral home when they closed the lid on Uncle Paul just before we started out. I begin to think someone has played a trick on us in the pink light of the viewing room. Surely there's more inside this casket than Uncle Paul: a couple of folding chairs, maybe an urn or two, the Hammond organ, another body from a different room, the crystal chandelier, a bag of salt waiting for the winter ice that will soon glaze the parking lot. Maybe death itself.

The incense startles me when the church doors open. I can't explain why I think the smells and sounds of Uncle Paul will be inside. I just want to be greeted, this last time, in this final place we'll ever be together, by the smell of dog, the strong odor of his golden retriever, its saliva everywhere, its urine tracking up the steps to the altar rail. Or by a priest who says something nice about my uncle Paul.

But this is his death, not mine, so I give him up. I rest the casket on the bier and watch the priest lower over it a white ecclesiastical pall embroidered with a cross of red and silver threads, and place a crucifix on top of that. I watch the whole thing roll down the center aisle. The pall, animated by the breeze, moves like a sheet upon a heaving chest.

He's no lighter after mass than he was before. It's even harder to get my uncle down the church stairs than up them. I still have to worry about dropping him, but now there's the height of the stairs as well as the weight of my uncle to consider. I could take a fall that would land *me* in a body cast. I could occupy the room he vacated in intensive care.

The last song we sang in church was "Lift Me Up on Angel Wings." I want the lightness that the words promised, but the only lightness is in my head and it fails to travel to any of my limbs. There's no gauze, no angel wings, no intercession. There are just my raw hands, little scoops of hands, and my thin legs struggling down those stairs, and autumn wind blowing hair into my eyes and fanning tears across my face—a delta where cheeks and chin and neck once had been. It's horrible and heavy and I hate it. I hate the final lift to place the casket on the track of green wheels that carries Uncle Paul into his dark chamber.

But he's on his way now. People have said goodbye, his body has been sprinkled by the priest through the coffin lid, the stories have been told about his smile, the beautification award he received from the city for flying his flag for fifty years, and his persistent comment in the hospital that green grass was growing on the ceiling of his room.

CHAPTER 37

He's leading the parade. We ride in the car right behind him all the way down Grant, from the church to the southern tip of the street in Firestone Park. We drive over the expressway first, then cross South Street, past DiFeo's Poultry, the old Borden building, the Southern Theater, and Shiloh Baptist Church. Then we cross Archwood Avenue and slow down at the 1300th block of Grant.

His flag isn't flying today. Of course not. If the flag were out, Uncle Paul would be alive, in his house eating his cornflakes, not in the hearse ahead of me.

The flag, the house, the street—all of it is disappearing now. The hearse is taking Grant Street with it in its wake. The street collapses in back of me, turns to water, dirt, and pure debris, and we begin to float. Uncle Paul's gray house crumbles, the porch falls in on itself, planks and boards spill into the rubble and mix with the Grant Street flood. And everything visible and invisible, everything that carries any weight—the street, the church, the park where he fell in love, the bakery and City Ice, Concordia Lutheran Church and St. Bernard's, the ledges and ravines, huge roots of trees, raspberries and rhubarb, tulips and *daf-nails,* my uncle's 9 C Florsheim shoes, the old Burkhardt Brewery, Crislips' Grocery Store, my uncle's family home where Ludwina lived, the Grant Street hill, Eddie's body lying on Cross and Grant, Grandpa disappearing down the street, Anna climbing the courthouse steps, his wife's screams, his son's, and his—everything is turned into a liquid stream that follows him.

So when I have to pick it up again, lift the casket to the cemetery plot, it seems as if every inch of Goosetown has been added to the weight. I'm surprised the box even looks the same when the back doors of the hearse open to let him out. I think that I'll find seaweed on the lid, gouges everywhere, a canvas mast lying limp where the pall has been, the handlebar ripped off, fish swimming in the chamber where the casket lies.

I have never felt such weight.

Up the hill we take the thing, and set it down.

It's over.

But the weight stays in my hands, the way it does when you've lifted something heavier than you are. My fingers and arms refuse to bend, locked in the shape of my uncle's casket.

I'm angry as I stand and hear the priest read the final words and watch him sprinkle holy water, sweetening Uncle Paul for one last time. He was old, but he left too soon. There are stories still waiting to be told and questions I have no answers to. But now he's gone.

He won't be coming back.

He's made me carry him around this hard day—cart him all over Goosetown and right to the grave. I never thought our last trip down Grant would look like this.

Soon there will be a marker above the body that they will bury here before the day is out. A small, flat stone the crew can mow around. I'll pry out the dandelions when they appear, but I don't think they'll grow for a year or two on this new sod.

Everything else will lie below.

When the deep sadness of this day begins to fade, I'll ask his son for my uncle's fountain pen, his postcard collection, one or two of his books.

Maybe the Bone Man will even give me a few pages from my uncle's journal.

That's all I want.

There was no money to disperse. Nothing in his estate. The house he lived in was quickly claimed by a son of his second wife.

I'm not in his will. It would surprise me if he even had one.

But I know what he's left me.

Goosetown no longer belongs to Uncle Paul.

He's given it to me.